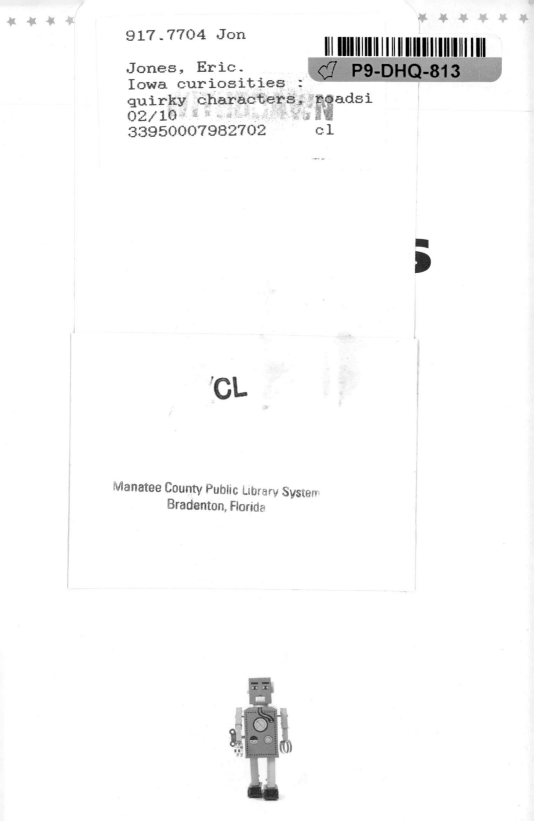

Help Us Keep This Guide Up to Date

Every effort has been made by the authors and editors to make this guide as accurate and useful as possible. However, many things can change after a guide is published—establishments close, phone numbers change, hiking trails are rerouted, facilities come under new management, etc.

We would love to hear from you concerning your experiences with this guide and how you feel it could be made better and be kept up to date. While we may not be able to respond to all comments and suggestions, we'll take them to heart and we'll also make certain to share them with the authors. Please send your comments and suggestions to the following address:

Globe Pequot Press
Reader Response/Editorial Department
P.O. Box 480
Guilford, CT 06437

Or you may e-mail us at:
editorial@GlobePequot.com

Thanks for your input, and happy travels!

Curiosities Series

Iowa CURIOSITIES

Quirky characters, roadside oddities & other offbeat stuff

Second Edition

Eric Jones and Dan Coffey with Berit Thorkelson

Guilford, Connecticut

The prices, rates, and hours listed in this guidebook were confirmed at press time. We recommend, however, that you call establishments to obtain current information before traveling.

To buy books in quantity for corporate use
or incentives, call **(800) 962–0973**
or e-mail **premiums@GlobePequot.com.**

Photos by the authors unless otherwise noted.

Maps by Daniel Lloyd copyright © Morris Book Publishing, LLC

Text design: Bret Kerr

Layout artist: Casey Shain

Project editor: John Burbidge

Library of Congress Cataloging-in-Publication data is available on file.

ISBN 978-0-7627-5419-9

Printed in the United States of America

10 9 8 7 6 5 4 3 2 1

contents

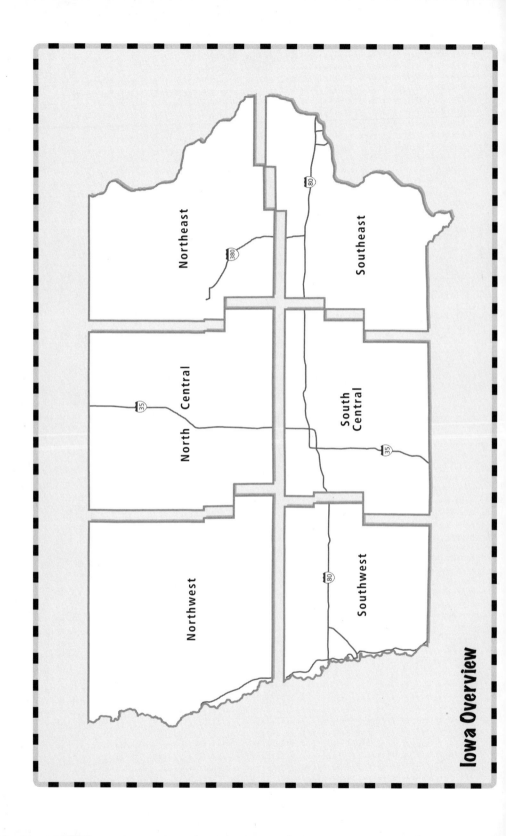

Iowa Overview

acknowledgments

*T*hanks to all those Iowans, from Sioux City to Muscatine and everywhere in between, who invited us into their homes, told us their stories, showed us collections, gave us impromptu history lessons—even fed us—and made a couple of characters, quirky in their own right, feel at home. We are additionally grateful to Berit Thorkelson, our intrepid guide to some of western Iowa's most curious attractions, including the world's largest Cheeto, displayed on its own handblown glass pedestal.

Thanks also to Angela Gray for her fantastic fact checking, and to Tony Gray for his visit to Bentonsport. For helpful suggestions, thanks to Lora Hansen, Abby Kisling, David Hockett, Paula Mohr, Rebecca Hess, Kari Burns, Cindy McGranahan, Jet Kofoot, Ken Purdy, David Hockett, Joanne Husack, Shirley Frederiksen, Stacey Reese, James Frisbie, Sue Meyer, Cheryl Duke, Shirley Phillips, Connie Street, Caroline Bredekamp, Ann McCurdy, and Shonna Bruno.

And finally our thanks to the staff at Globe Pequot Press for their support and unflagging patience.

introduction

Oddity is in the eye of the beholder.

I traveled out east a few years ago in a 1997 Geo Prizm with Johnson County, Iowa, plates. Not long after crossing into New Hampshire on I-95, I noticed a father and son on a motorcycle pulling up alongside us to pass. Even though I was paying close attention to the road ahead, my hands at ten and two o'clock on the wheel, knuckles just the slightest bit pale (East Coast driving can be a little more demanding than Corn Belt driving), I couldn't help but notice that the pair was passing us very, very slowly. What's more, I had that uncanny but unmistakable feeling that I was being watched. Sure enough, when I looked to my left, both pop and progeny were staring at us from behind the visors of their helmets with a wide-eyed curiosity that made me feel a bit like an exhibit at the zoo. "I saw them staring at us from way back," my companion told me. "I think they were looking at our Iowa plates."

And so it was that by driving 1,127 miles east, my companion and I, our small black sedan, and its license plate with the gray outline of a farmyard beneath the vague silhouette of a city skyline and a patch of baby blue sky, had become Iowa curiosities. "I hope you got a good close look, son," I imagined the father saying at their next rest stop. "That couple in the Geo, they were from Ohio." And I imagined the son looking up at his father and asking, "Isn't that where they grow all those potatoes?"

If you've spent much time on either coast, you know that for most Americans Iowa is more a hazy idea than a reality, more symbol than actual state. When it's not confused with Idaho or Ohio, two other states with what my Connecticut friend likes to call "skewed vowel-to-consonant ratios," Iowa means small towns, farms, corn, covered bridges, and not a whole lot else. In fact, it seems to come as a bit of a shock to coastal denizens that people, real people, actually live here. "Iowa?" the Californian will bellow incredulously when he meets you, as if Iowa is another Timbuktu. "Who lives in Iowa?" Or worse, a New Yorker might ask you in earnest, "Why do you live in Iowa?" with more than a hint of pity in her voice, as if settling in West Des Moines were akin to living on a Russian space station.

introduction

I'm not complaining, though, at least not too loudly. After all, one of the main reasons Midwesterners travel in the first place is to be strangers for a while, to make our ordinary selves a little more exotic than we have a right to be, and then pleasantly or not so pleasantly bump up against the ways we're misunderstood. Being an Iowan in New York City or in Paris feels different than being an Iowan in Cedar Rapids, and it's partly that unfamiliar way of being ourselves that we travelers seek out.

Mostly, though, we hit the road in search of the new, the strange, and the extraordinary in this great big world. We leave home to discover something our neighbors haven't ever seen before, take pictures of it, and bring the evidence back home for show-and-tell. We head out to be impressed. And although some people think you need to cross whole continents and wide blue seas to see things you've never seen, or even imagined, while researching this book we discovered that oddity is a lot closer to home than you might think.

So what curiosities did we find in our own backyard? How about a life-size concrete pink elephant wearing a top hat? Or a Guinness-certified world's second-largest collection of salt and pepper shakers (more than 14,000 and counting)? And what about a man who turned a grain silo into a five-story house, or a contest where the players throw cast-iron skillets at scarecrows, or a Trappist monastery where the monks build coffins for their daily bread? In the next county over, maybe even just across town, down a dirt road you've never taken, you'll find all the oddity you're looking for and more.

So here's to quirkiness close at hand. Here's to all the ways we can be surprised by what we thought we knew just by driving a little farther and taking a closer look. Seeking out the unfamiliar isn't for the faint-hearted. It takes courage to leave the couch and say hello to a stranger, particularly a stranger who's on the strange side. And the world's biggest anything can be scary, even if it's something as seemingly harmless as an overpuffed Cheeto. Dear readers, fellow travelers, soon-to-be strangers, we know you're up to the challenge. Enjoy!

—Eric Jones

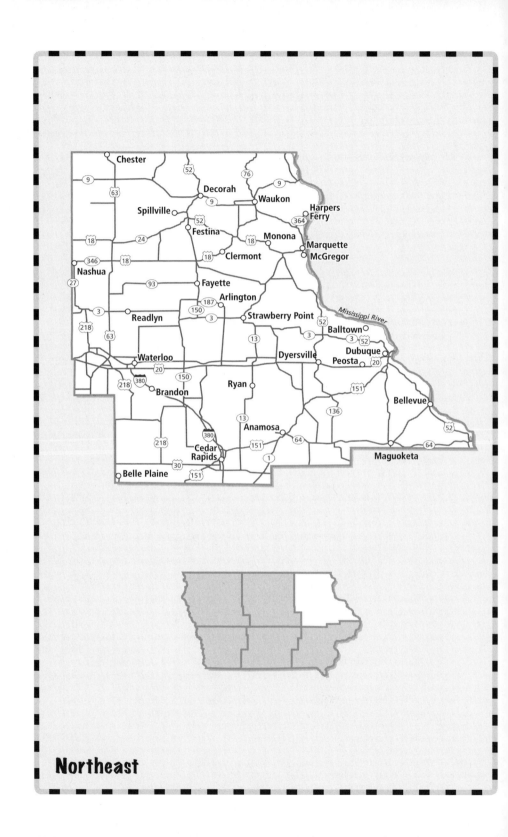

Chester
52
76
9
9
63
Decorah
Waukon
9
Harpers
Ferry
Spillville
52
364
Festina
Monona
18
Marquette
18
McGregor
18
Clermont
346
18
Nashua
27
93
Fayette
Arlington
187
Strawberry Point
Mississippi River
Readlyn
150
3
52
218
3
Balltown
63
13
3
52
Waterloo
Dyersville
Dubuque
20
Peosta
20
218
380
150
Brandon
Ryan
151
218
136
Bellevue
380
13
52
218
Anamosa
64
Cedar
151
64
Rapids
64
Maguoketa
30
1
Belle Plaine
151

Northeast

1

Northeast

If you're from out of state, you're probably expecting Iowa to be flat, like Kansas or a pancake. The Northeast section of the state is a good place to derail that expectation: There are hills all over, and, generally speaking, the more northeast you go in the Northeast, the hillier it gets.

One of the most devastating losses in the Northeast's history occurred between the book's 2005 edition and this one: the flooding of nearly 10 square miles of Cedar Rapids in June of 2008. The Cedar River crested at 31 feet, more than 10 feet higher than the crest during the Great Flood of 1993, which some experts had called the single biggest natural disaster in U.S. history. The rebuilding from the 2008 flood goes on.

On a happier note, the mini replica of the Statue of Liberty in Cedar Rapids is a favorite new addition. There are replicas of Lady Liberty all over the state, but this one takes the cake, especially because she sits right over the Cedar River but somehow made it through the flood just fine. Iowa's largest fryin' pan is just off the road in Brandon; you can down your lutefisk really fast at Decorah's Norwegian Fest and not hurt Grandma Bjornsen's feelings—first one done's the winner in a lutefisk-eating contest; and finally, Breitbach's up in Balltown, the oldest bar and restaurant in Iowa, burned down not once, but twice in a little under a year. They're rebuilding again, and scheduled to reopen before this edition goes to print. Go eat there. Seriously. And give Mike Breitbach and everyone in town who volunteered to help rebuild not once, but twice a great big pat on the back.

★ ★

Play Prisoner for a Day Right Beside 1,200 Inmates
Anamosa

Iowa's own version of Alcatraz is the Anamosa State Penitentiary, a maximum-security facility housing more than 1,200 inmates. Built in 1872 from local limestone, the prison is an architectural manifestation of deep depression: Fortress-style stone walls the color of overcast sky rise up, and up, and up, high enough to contain four tiers of barred cells, one on top of another, in open cell blocks as long as football fields. As tantalizing a place as it sounds, you can't tour the penitentiary building without either a good reason or a heavy debt to society, but you can visit the Anamosa State Penitentiary Museum to get a taste of life in Anamosa's big house over the past century and a half.

Located beside the penitentiary in a converted outbuilding that once housed a cheese factory, the Anamosa Museum is a small treasure trove of information about the prison's construction, famous and not-so-famous inmates, guards, and prison life. One highlight is a replica of an old prison cell: Step inside, slam the door, and try not to scream when someone says "life sentence." Truth be told, the real penitentiary with its living, breathing inmates may be a bit too close for comfort to take much pleasure in playing convict—a sign alongside the prison driveway even asks visitors to lock their car doors before they enter so that escaping inmates can't make an easy getaway.

The museum has archived loads of information about some less-than-savory characters, including Wesley Elkins, an eleven-year-old boy who served a life sentence at Anamosa for murdering his parents in 1889, first shooting his father in his bed and then, unable to find wadding to reload the rifle, bludgeoning his stepmother to death with a club. And do you remember John Wayne Gacy, one of the most notorious serial killers in U.S. history? Convicted in 1980 of murdering thirty-three young men, Gacy spent two years at the penitentiary in the 1960s and was reportedly a model prisoner.

A big house with surprisingly cramped rooms.

It may not be the most cheery weekend activity, but a visit to Anamosa's prison museum will delight crime and punishment fans and history buffs alike. Just be sure to check the backseat before you leave the parking lot.

Open Friday, Saturday, and Sunday from noon to 4:00 p.m. Other times are by appointment. The museum's phone number is (319) 462-2386 or visit www.asphistory.com.

5,300 Hats (and Counting) and a Money Pit
Arlington

Faith Mitchell, a local farm wife, began collecting hats decades ago and over the years acquired hundreds upon hundreds of caps, bonnets, and fedoras from places as far-flung as Spain, Germany, and

★ ★

China. In 1987 she and her family, owners of Mitchell's House of Hats, donated her vast collection to the Castle House Preservation Society, or CHPS, a local nonprofit working to preserve and restore a local Queen Ann–style home with a castlelike clapboard turret in serious disrepair. So serious, in fact, that in between the last edition of this book and the current one, CHPS had to cry uncle and sell their beloved painted (and peeling very badly) lady and relocate Mitchell's wonderful collection to a vacant storefront on Main Street.

Still, it was the collection and not the house that was the thing, and the sheer variety of hats is astounding. Bertha Schuchmann and a few other CHPS volunteers indexed and affixed labels to a good many of the hats, which range from simple bonnets and classic top hats from the late nineteenth century to wild, flowery affairs that would have done any 1920s Chicago flapper proud. Racks and racks of hats fill the space, with manufacturers and designers including Christian Dior, Alice May of Fifth Avenue, and Montgomery Ward.

People keep donating hats to the collection, so if you're looking for baseball caps, you'll find some of those, too, as well as a cap affixed with a beer-can holder at each temple and two curled straws intended for the hat-owner's mouth. But, surely, this was a recent addition—judging from the bulk of the collection, Faith Mitchell had far more refined tastes in headwear.

Since the collection's location could change again, call either Bertha Schuchmann at (563) 633-3385 or Alice Miller at (563) 633-5492 to make an appointment and get directions. (Both serve as tour guides, and both knew Faith Mitchell personally.) Arlington is located on IA 187, about 5 miles north of IA 3.

Where Diners Outnumber the Locals Four to One
Balltown

Food-savvy travelers know a good test of any wayside restaurant is whether or not the locals eat there. See only out-of-county plates in the lot, and you may want to keep hunting for native diners—unless you happen to be in Balltown, that is. Perched on a bluff high above the Mississippi and offering truly spectacular views of the river valley below, Balltown has a population listed at approximately sixty-four people, or twenty families, about the size of your average high school football team. Even if half the town dined out for every meal, they wouldn't be so easy to track down.

Not to fear. There's only one restaurant in town, and the food there is very good. Breitbach's, which lays claim to the title of oldest bar and restaurant in Iowa, has seating for four times Balltown's population. On the busiest days, owner Mike Breitbach says, "We can serve more than thirteen, fourteen hundred people." And trying to find the locals in a crowd like that is a whole lot harder than finding Waldo.

Jacob Breitbach, Mike's great-great-grandfather, purchased the 1852 tavern in 1891, and it's been in the Breitbach family ever since. (Mike and his wife, Cindy, are almost always at the restaurant to greet you and invite you to sign the guest book.) The restaurant used to contain some real treasures from great-great-grandpa Breitbach's day, including a horse blanket left in the livery stable by one Frank James, Jesse James's clearly forgetful brother. Jacob actually had the foresight to take a picture of the James gang when they stopped in at Breitbach's back in 1876, and the old photograph used to hang on the wall. Two recent fires, one on Christmas Eve of 2007 and the second on October 24, 2008, destroyed the restaurant twice, along with the many antiques and collectibles that once lined the walls, including my personal favorite, a Depression-era mural depicting the same splendid view of the Mississippi you can see just out the back door, painted by a wandering gypsy named Alberto in return for food and lodging.

Breitbach's is scheduled for a midsummer 2009 reopening. At this point, wall decorations haven't been chosen, but with not one, but two devastating fires in ten months, who could blame Mike and Cindy Breitbach if they forgo the antiques and collectibles and simply

festoon the walls with hundreds upon hundreds of fire extinguishers?

Take US 52 out of Dubuque to Sageville and then follow the Great River Road into Balltown. Breitbach's will be on the right. During the summer season Breitbach's is open for breakfast, lunch, and dinner seven days a week. In the winter it's closed Monday. For information and reservations, call (563) 552-2220.

The Geyser Downtown

Belle Plaine

For better or worse, towns usually don't get to choose their claims to fame. Sure, it's nice to be home to a famous athlete, or Nobel Prize winner, or even a politician, in a pinch, but all towns can't be so lucky. Belle Plaine's moment (or months) in the international spotlight arrived on August 26, 1886, when an artesian well dug by William Weir & Sons spouted water 53 feet in the air and kept on flowing unchecked for the next fourteen months. News reports from the time claim the well was "vomiting out a stream as large as the fore wheel of a wagon," and though we're not sure how big a fore wheel is, we know it's got to be a whole lot bigger than a breadbox, but maybe smaller than the back wheel of a wagon.

One thing is certain about the well, aptly christened Jumbo: It sent a whole lot of water into Belle Plaine. According to experts, Jumbo Well spewed more than 5 million gallons of water daily, or about 3,500 gallons per minute, which, in case you were curious, calculates to about 60 gallons a second. (Try taking a sip from the flow, and the phrase "a stiff drink" would gain a whole new meaning.)

And as the water kept on flowing, Belle Plaine's fame grew. Tourists from around the country and around the world came to see Jumbo, bought postcards of the gusher (now only 6 or 7 feet high, at least in the postcard we saw) and commemorative Jumbo Well rocks, and did whatever else one did in nineteenth-century Belle Plaine.

In spite of the benefits of the friendly visitors and their greenbacks, Belle Plaine's citizens still wanted their five-million-gallon-a-day spigot

You wouldn't know it now, but this quiet corner was once home to a very stubborn geyser.

shut off, so they brought in experts from Chicago and beyond to help, but no one was successful. Ultimately, a local company, Palmer Brothers Foundry, capped Jumbo on October 6, 1887, using a contraption composed of two metal pipes, one inside the other, and a whole lot of gravel and concrete. (Don't ask us how it worked; we're not engineers.)

The place where Jumbo Well once gushed is now a quiet, shady street corner in a residential neighborhood a couple of blocks from downtown Belle Plaine, with the well site marked by a large boulder and plaque. The town also honors its artesian heritage with a yearly fall festival called Jumbo Days, featuring a cemetery walk (more festive than you might think), a Fly-In Breakfast at the local airport, and a hot-air-balloon liftoff. And though a gusher that bubbled on and on and on is not a terrible thing to be famous for, a movie-

star daughter or an astronaut son would have been a lot less of a headache.

The Jumbo Well boulder and plaque is located on the corner of Eighth Street and Eighth Avenue in Belle Plaine. Jumbo Days is held the last weekend in September. For more information, contact the Belle Plaine Historical Society at (319) 434-6093.

A Pit Stop at Your Great-Grandfather's Gas Station
Belle Plaine

The Old Lincoln Highway, the first transcontinental roadway in the United States, began in New York, ended in San Francisco 3,331 long and dusty miles later, and passed right through little Belle Plaine along the way. If you want to get a good feel for what it was like to make a pit stop for gas along the Lincoln Highway some eighty years

You can't fill 'er up here, but take a gander at those signs. Catherine Cole

★ ★

ago, take 21 North about three blocks out of town, put your right-turn blinker on, and ease the old jalopy into George Preston's gas station and garage. No brightly lit convenience store filled with 3,000 kinds of confectionary delights, no pay-at-the-pump convenience here, just a one-bay wooden garage and, next to it, the tiny office with two old gas pumps out front, all looking pretty much the way they did back in the 1920s, save for a little graying and weathering to let you know it's all real, not some museum reproduction.

The old gas pump is worth the visit all by itself—towering almost 10 feet into the air, it looks something like a miniature lighthouse with a long black hose attached—but George Preston has also covered his station walls with hundreds of oil and gas signs from the last century. In addition to the more familiar Shell, Pennzoil, Texaco, and Mobil logos, there are signs for Red Crown (picturing a brilliant red crown, of course), Wadhams, and Nevrnox gasoline. They're a collector's fantasy and a credit to Iowa honesty and uprightness that they haven't been taken under cover of darkness and auctioned off on eBay.

Be sure to stop inside the office, too. There's an old register, fifty-year-old unopened oil cans on the shelves, newspaper clippings featuring George grinning wide for the camera beside his station, actual chunks of the old highway on the windowsill (the labels stuck on with duct tape), a poster listing the hundreds of towns the Old Lincoln Highway passed through, and even more signs, ones offering cheery road advice such as "Dim your lights behind a car, let folks see how bright you are." Stop for five minutes and spend half the afternoon, as we did. Just don't blame us if you feel deep twinges of nostalgia for the good old days the next time you fill 'er up on the interstate.

Preston's gas station is at the intersection of Fourth and Thirteenth Streets, Belle Plaine.

★ ★

Read 'Em, Weep, and Call the Movers

Bellevue

Although this decidedly upscale bed-and-breakfast, located on a nine-acre wooded bluff overlooking the Mississippi, has a lot to recommend it, including a breathtaking view, twelve beautifully appointed guest rooms, and more Jacuzzi tubs than a California spa, its most notable charm is its checkered past.

When a wealthy land developer named Seth Luellyn Baker built the home in 1893, its unique architectural feature was a round third-floor tower room, accessible only by stepping onto the roof of the building and then climbing through a hatch. The room's purpose? High-stakes, invitation-only, illegal (because transpiring on land) poker matches, conducted safe from the intrusions of the local authorities.

Mont Rest quickly grew infamous for its late-night gambling, and it was in one of these heavyweights-only poker matches in 1895, just two years after the home was built, that Seth Baker, short of cash,

Does anyone know the number for Gamblers Anonymous?

called a $6,000 bet with the deed to his house. Oh, and did I mention Seth Baker had a wife, a woman who probably considered the house hers, too? After his opponent lay his cards on the table, Mr. Baker is reported to have excused himself, climbed out the hatch, then walked across the roof and down the stairs to tell his beloved they had two weeks to pack up and move out. (Do you think they had couples therapy back in 1895?)

The gambling room underwent a conversion of sorts in the early twentieth century, when an eccentric owner named Frank Weinshank set up an altar and heard daily Mass in the tower from a local priest. One of Weinshank's more eccentric acts, in a lifetime filled with kookiness, was filing a lawsuit against Bell Telephone for religious persecution for refusing to lay a transatlantic phone line from Mont Rest to the Vatican in Rome so that he could have a direct line to the pope. You don't need to be a Supreme Court justice to know his case had a few holes in it.

To top it all off, from the fifties until the late seventies, Mont Rest and the Tower Room, as it's now called, stood abandoned: Animals took up residence, vandals smashed windows, and the woods encroached on the property. As recently as 1979, the *Des Moines Register* ran a story about the so-called Haunted Castle of Bellevue, which loomed on the north bluff overlooking town.

Today Mont Rest is arguably one of the most luxurious bed-and-breakfasts in the region. Guests can reserve the Tower Room if they're looking for privacy, a sweeping view of the river, rich history, a double shower, and just outside on the roof where gamblers once strode, a seven-person hot tub. Seth Baker, even when he was on the winning side of the table, probably never had it so good.

Bellevue is located midway between Clinton and Dubuque on US 52 (the Great River Road). Mont Rest's address is 300 Spring Street, right on the bluff three blocks north of downtown. Christine Zraick, the innkeeper, can be reached toll-free at (877) 872-4220 or (563) 872-4220, or visit www.montrest.com.

A Pan for the Masses

Brandon

After a vacation in Canada, former Brandon mayor Ron Boyer came home with a big idea. Or, to put it more precisely, he came home with the idea of something big. He just wasn't sure what that something big should be.

On their northern travels he and his wife happened to pass the world's largest buffalo, a 26-foot-tall concrete sculpture with its least flattering side to the highway, in Jamestown, North Dakota, and

Where's the oversized spatula?

★ ★

started thinking seriously about getting the tiny little town of Brandon something very big to call its own.

But what? Inspired by example, the couple started brainstorming about a giant locally appropriate animal, along the lines of Albert, Audubon's towering bull, or Nevis, Minnesota's world's largest muskie. Since Iowa is the hog capital of the world, why not a giant hog? they thought. But for some reason, a concrete pig towering Godzilla-like over his neighbors' rooftops didn't seem quite right to Mayor Boyer, and that's when inspiration hit: Why not give Brandon its own jumbo kettle in honor of the town's twice-annual Cowboy Breakfast fund-raiser? The kettle soon became a frying pan for ease of execution, and the only thing left for Boyer to do was to round up seven or eight local volunteers to help him hammer (and cut and weld and paint) out the details.

Boyer and his cohorts cut the pan out of an old 5,000-gallon steel chemical tank that he had been planning to fill with manure, using a little 10-inch fryer as a model. The end result, after what Boyer reports was "quite a bit of welding," is a pretty darn authentic-looking frying pan standing over 10 feet tall and weighing in at 1,040 pounds with the words BRANDON, IOWA painted in white across the front. Little Brandon had gotten its own very big thing.

People come from all around to see the pan and stand up close for a picture, which is pretty much the whole point behind a small town building an oversize anything, whether it be beast, fish, or culinary tool: to convince people who are busy trying to get someplace else (maybe even *anyplace* else) to stop and take notice. When I asked Boyer just how many people the pan brings in, he said, "Now I'm not really bragging, but on summer weekends almost every time you drive by there's a different car stopped with people looking at it and taking pictures."

The high traffic is thanks in part to a slam-dunk marketing campaign out on I-380. "I had some land along the interstate and a friend had land on the other side, and we found out that if we zoned

★ ★

50 square feet commercial each, we could put signs up for the pan," Boyer said. Exits for small towns are easy to miss, but the signs proclaiming Brandon home to Iowa's largest fryin' pan really do coax the masses into town, if only for a brief visit and a fill-up at the Kwik Stop. "I've driven all around the country, and you don't really see signs like that along the interstate," Boyer told me. I had to agree: Interstate signs advertising very large pans are indeed quite rare. But now it really did sound as if he were bragging just a little.

Brandon is midway between Cedar Rapids and Waterloo on I-380. After you see the above-mentioned signs, take exit 49 and head approximately 1 mile west into town. Of course, it should go without saying that you can't miss the pan.

The Secret Is in the Sauce
Cedar Rapids

Whether he was maintaining journalistic objectivity or not, a reporter from the *Chicago Sun Times* once noted, "Searching for the best soul food in Iowa is like looking for a square dance in Harlem." Well, he obviously didn't look too hard in Cedar Rapids, because Al & Irene's has long been the place to go in eastern Iowa for anyone seeking a soul-food fix.

Al and Irene Quarterman claim their family barbecue sauce dates back more than seventy years; they slather it on chicken, pork, back ribs, spareribs, beef ribs, and even turkey, and then they serve it up right, with a healthy dollop of coleslaw. Save some room for dessert, too—they make their own delectable pies from scratch. So where exactly did you say that square dance was in Harlem?

Al & Irene's is located east of I-380 near Blair's Ferry Road at 2020 North Towne Lane NE. Hours of operation are Tuesday through Saturday from 11:00 a.m. to 9:00 p.m., Sunday 11:00 a.m. to 5:00 p.m., and Monday 11:00 a.m. to 8:00 p.m. For more information, call (319) 393-6242.

Barbecue this good will make you feel like you've died and gone to Chicago.

A Little Bit of Liberty Never Hurt Anybody

Cedar Rapids

Drive around Iowa long enough looking for weird stuff, and you're sure to notice that miniature replicas of the Statue of Liberty are popular civic statuary, posted on pedestals in town squares and in front of county courthouses all across the state: Burlington, Cedar Falls, Davenport, Des Moines, Dubuque, and Fort Dodge all have a mini Lady Liberty, as do Independence, Mount Pleasant, Muscatine, Sioux City, and a score of others. They stand about 8 feet tall and bear a striking resemblance to the original (who measures a whopping 151 feet from tip of toe to top of torch), though some people point out that the faces of the replicas look doughier and more childlike than the original, perhaps to suggest that they're the Statue of Liberty's offspring on a 1:20 scale.

★ ★

A little lady to make us all proud. Will Jennings

All told, there are over 200 of these little daughters of liberty all around the country (with one even as far away as Guam, the little adventurous wanderer . . .), but with more than twenty-five to call its own, Iowa has more than its fair share. It's as if the little gals were given a choice where to live and a sizable number picked Iowa, which, we're told, can be confused with heaven. (At least during the four weeks out of the year when the weather is just right.)

Manufactured in Chicago and sold through the Kansas City Boy Scout office to commemorate Scouting's fortieth anniversary in 1950, the copper statues cost $350 plus freight, base not included. Towns simply had to pick a spot, construct a base, and, voila, they had their very own French-designed symbol of American freedom and democracy.

Cedar Rapids' pint-size Liberty might just be the best of the lot, not because she's any different (she's not), but because she stands with her tiny torch upthrust on the First Avenue bridge crossing the Cedar River, overlooking the city's municipal buildings on May's Island. (Cedar Rapids claims the unique honor of being the only city in the world other than Paris to have its municipal buildings on an island in the city's center.) During the flood of 2008, the bridge itself was completely submerged, but somehow little Liberty made it through.

Of course, water is the perfect backdrop for the Statue of Liberty's copper robes and gleaming torch. And even if a small Lady Liberty on a little bridge over the brown and placid waters of the Cedar River is a far cry from New York Harbor, it's still enough to make you feel more than a little proud that this vision, or something like this vision, is what greeted immigrants to America for generations.

The Statue of Liberty replica is located in downtown Cedar Rapids on the First Avenue bridge.

How Strange, a Prairie in Iowa
Chester

It may seem strange, but in a place that used to be nothing but prairie, people can now live their whole lives without ever seeing one. The flowers and prairie grass that at one time blanketed the state grew so high that, as one nineteenth-century soldier-explorer said, you could tie the stalks together over the back of a horse.

In the prairie's stead, of course, we now have hundreds of thousands of acres of corn, soy, and oats that eventually end up in everything from breakfast cereals to soft drinks to internal-combustion engines. But as beautiful as those rows and rows of corn can be—the

★ ★

Bet you never thought you'd see a real prairie in Iowa.

way the gaps between the stalks suddenly open into slivers of shadow and then just as quickly close as you're driving by—the prairie is the Iowa countryside's wilder, more extravagant incarnation.

If you've never seen a prairie, be sure to visit 240-acre Hayden Prairie, one of the largest in the state. The parcel of land is really the size of a single small farm, but it's big enough that if you walk far enough out into the tall grasses, the gravel roads and fences disappear from view, and you can easily imagine what it was like here 160 years ago, when pioneers started the backbreaking work of turning prairie into farmland. Though the countless varieties of flowers and grasses blooming and growing—from big bluestem to purple prairie clover to yellow star grass—will vary with the season, the prairie is profligate, and wildly beautiful, from early spring to autumn. Just a word of caution from our lawyers, though: Tying prairie grass around a horse's back is not recommended by the authors, as serious injuries, and grass stains, could result.

Hayden Prairie is a few miles south of Chester on CR V26.

A One-Horse, Two-Tractor Town

Clermont

This small town, population 716, is blessed with not one, but two famous (at least by Iowa standards) tractors. Both sit conveniently on Main Street about one block apart in small, simple wooden buildings with large plate-glass windows facing the street for easy viewing. There's no admission charge, no lines, and the night we visited, not a single other adult downtown, just three kids playing tag in the middle of the quiet street.

The first, and perhaps most famous, tractor is the green 1966 John Deere riding lawn mower and absurdly large attached trailer (complete with a small set of antlers up front) featured in the 1999 David Lynch film, *The Straight Story*. (The real, original Straight tractor is in Laurens. See "A Lawnmower Ride with Friends" in chapter 5.) Based on a true story, the film chronicles the adventures of Alvin Straight, a seventy-three-year-old retiree from Laurens, Iowa, who, having lost his driver's license because of poor eyesight, decides to drive his lawn mower more than 240 miles across two states to visit his estranged and ailing brother in Mount Zion, Wisconsin. Along the way he meets a pregnant runaway, a fellow World War II vet, and a priest, among others, and there's plenty of heartwarming straight talk between Alvin and his fellow Iowans. When someone asks why he's driving a tractor, at a top speed of 5 miles per hour, all the way to Wisconsin, he says simply, "My eyes are bad. I can't drive. I don't like someone else driving. And I've got to get out to my brother." Spoken like a true Iowan.

The second tractor, though less famous, is still impressive. It's a 1927 Hart Parr manufactured in Charles City, Iowa. The rusting machine sits on a faded purple shag carpet (a keepsake from the tractor's 1970s disco phase?) looking exactly like what it is: a very old tractor. The manufacturer of the machine, Hart Parr, is famous for having coined the term *tractor* when the company shortened the old name for the machines, gasoline traction engines. The information

★ ★

posted beside the tractor kindly explains that it has a two-cylinder, four-cycle, horizontal valve in-head engine, and if you know what that means, then you're either a farmer or a good candidate for a very old tractor repair school.

The tractors are located on Main Street (US 18) in downtown Clermont.

Lutefisk: It's What's for Dinner!
Decorah

If you go to Decorah's annual Nordic Fest at the end of July, there are a number of competitive events you could enter, including both a 5K and 10K road race, a canoe race called Kanolopet (is that Norwegian for "paddle harder"?), and a rock throw. But if you really want to test your Scandinavian mettle, you should save your strength, and your stomach, for the lutefisk-eating contest.

If you have to ask, "What's a lutefisk?" you might be at a distinct disadvantage. It seems most entrants have been eating the aromatic concoction of dried cod (or other whitefish) soaked in a water and lye solution since they were small and impressionable Norwegian-Americans, and they've developed either a taste or a high tolerance for it—it's hard to say which.

Well-prepared lutefisk, if we can be generous for a moment, sup-posedly has a mild taste that calls for seasoning or sauce, but I lack the courage to be able to confirm or deny this. No matter how well-prepared, lutefisk has the consistency of jelly (fish jelly, that is) and, if made from cod instead of pollack or haddock, a pungent and unfor-gettable odor. Garrison Keillor once said of lutefisk: "Most lutefisk is not edible by normal people. It is reminiscent of the afterbirth of a dog or the world's largest chunk of phlegm." Well now, don't those metaphors just make your mouth water?

And therein lies the fun, and the challenge, of a lutefisk-eating contest. The first contestant to finish his or her plastic bowl of lutefisk is proclaimed the winner, and eating styles range from focused to furious. According to the *Decorah Journal,* the winner in 2008, a nineteen-year-old from Ames named Sarah Schreitmueller, slurped down two full bowls on her way to victory and then, post-contest, stood in line for a third helping. "I couldn't wish for anything better," she reportedly said. Now that, my friends, is either a true champion or a bona fide glutton for punishment.

Decorah celebrates its Nordic Fest in late July each year. For more information, go to www.nordicfest.com or call (800) 382-FEST. And if you're worried about the eats at the festival, don't despair: As if to make up for the lutefisk, the rest of the Scandinavian fare offered, including things like *lefse* and *rommegrot* and *kranskake,* are sundry concoctions made from sugar, flour, cream, and butter.

Help! Help! Rescue That Seed!
Decorah

Ever try a Cherokee Purple Tomato or a White Wonder Cucumber? Ever sampled Jimmy Nardello's Sweet Italian Frying Peppers (that's quite a mouthful); sunk your teeth into a delicious ear of Bloody Butcher Corn, with its dark, wine-red kernels; or tasted some Rattle-snake Snap Beans? If your answers are no, no, no, no, and no, it's not surprising, especially if you pick your veggies from the local mega-grocery-store produce aisles, where hybrid vegetables bred to with-stand long hauls from places as far away as New Zealand and Chile are the norm. (Them skins are made for transcontinental shipping.)

All of the above qualify as heirlooms, rare varieties of vegetables, fruits, and grains handed down within families of gardeners for gen-erations. But unlike the family jewels, these heirlooms are available to everyone, from weekend gardeners to commercial growers, in a free catalog published by the Seed Saver's Exchange, a Decorah-based nonprofit dedicated to saving more than 11,000 endangered varieties of garden seeds from extinction. Founded in 1975, the Seed Saver's

★ ★

Help! Save that purple tomato!

Exchange, or SSE, has more than 8,000 members, some of whom grow their own heirloom varieties and make the seeds available to the SSE and the public.

The Seed Saver's Exchange also owns and operates the beautiful 170-acre Heritage Farm near Decorah, which serves as heirloom-vegetable patch, rare-fruit orchard, and headquarters for the organization. They offer daily tours of both Preservation Gardens and Historic Orchard throughout the growing season, where visitors might see such colorful varieties as Boothby's Blonde Cucumbers, Applegreen Eggplants, or Black Sea Man Tomatoes. You may want to visit in mid to late July, when the gardens are literally bursting with fruits and vegetables, many of which have longer pedigrees than Kentucky thoroughbreds. But before you go, be forewarned: All those poor endangered plants can really tug at the old heartstrings. If you're tempted to save a threatened variety by buying twenty-five pounds of, say, Taponica Striped Maize seed (those purple stripes on the corn leaves are beautiful, aren't they?), you could regret it come planting time.

The Seed Saver's Exchange Heritage Farm Visitor Center, 3076 North Winn Road, is open April through December only. Hours are Monday through Friday from 9:00 a.m. to 5:00 p.m., Saturday and Sunday 10:00 a.m. to 5:00 p.m. From the junction of IA 9 and US 52, drive 5.5 miles north on US 52. Turn right on North Winn Road (W-34) and proceed 1 mile to the visitor parking sign. Call (563) 382-5990 for more information.

For the Love of the Nap

Dubuque

Though Dubuque's Fenelon Place Elevator, or Fourth Street Elevator, as it's also known, may just possibly be the steepest, shortest railroad in the world, it's most certainly the only railroad ever built so that a person could enjoy an afternoon nap.

In 1882 it took Dubuque resident J. K. Graves, a former mayor and Iowa senator, about half an hour to drive his horse and buggy from his home on top of the bluffs to the bank where he worked at the bottom, even though the actual distance between the two was the equivalent of a mere two-and-a-half very, very steep blocks, straight down the bluff. With only an hour and a half for lunch, Mr. Graves didn't have enough time to get up the bluff, eat his lunch, take his preferred half-hour nap, and get back to the bank for business. (I know what you're thinking: Poor, poor Mr. Graves. Why doesn't he try scarfing down a ham sandwich bought from a vending machine as he sits multitasking in some windowless cubicle like the rest of us?)

Instead of buying a faster horse, Graves decided to build a 296-foot cable-car line to pull him up and down the 189-foot-high bluff. Mr. Graves's horse put in for early retirement on July 24, 1882; the cable car operated for the first time the following day; and a mere few days later (or so it must have seemed), J. K. Graves's neighbors began pestering him to ride the elevator, too. He opened the elevator

The view from the top of the Fenelon Place Elevator. Catherine Cole

to the public in 1884, charging 5 cents a ride, and soon townspeople were depending on it to get them to work, to church, to school, and to their own afternoon naps.

The bluff is steep, the ride is pleasantly slow, and the view of the city and the river beyond opens up very, very quickly as you ascend. If you enter from the bottom of the bluff, at Fourth Street, you simply get on the car, ring the bell, and wait to ascend; you pay the small fare at the operator's house up top, where there's also a deck for enjoying the view. But, alas, there's no lunch waiting for you, as there would have been for Graves, and there's certainly no bed available to the public for napping. Could someone at least pass a Lunchable?

The Fenelon Place Elevator is located at 512 Fenelon Place, on top of the bluff overlooking town. You can also board a car from Fourth

Street, at the bottom of the bluff, and then pay at the top. The elevator is open April through November, 8:00 a.m. to 10:00 p.m. For
more information, call (563) 582-6496 or visit www.dbq.com/fenplco.

Check Out Them Checkers
Dubuque

Don Deweber, creator and curator of the World of Checkers Museum
(which also doubles as his apartment), is that special breed of collector who turns an obsession into a way of life. "I've gone without
many meals just so I could buy books on checkers," he told me. "I'm
what you call a bibliomaniac: I had over 20,000 checker books before
I donated them to Loras [a private college in Dubuque] and the
Cleveland Public Library."

While books on checkers are his first passion, or more accurately,
his first monomania, he recognizes that they're not necessarily everyone's cup of tea. "They're not the kind of book you read for fun, like
Little Red Riding Hood. They're about checkers strategy, just descrip-
tions, really, of what we call 'lines of play' from famous matches."
And with an estimated 500 billion billion possible situations that
could arise in a match (I'm not joking here), there's seemingly no end
to checkers strategy, nor the books that one could write about it.

That's just fine with Deweber, otherwise known as Mr. Checkers.
"*Lee's Guide to the Game of Checkers* was first published in 1897,
and I had over 500 copies of that book representing 127 different
editions. Not many collectors would do that." Indeed. It's widely
believed that his collection of books on checkers was possibly the
largest and almost certainly the most complete in the entire world.

But Mr. Checkers' passion for checkers didn't stop with books. Over
the last thirty years, he's filled his tidy apartment with every checkers
set imaginable (made of everything from wood to Bakelite to bone), as
well as an impressive variety of checkers memorabilia: His kitchen cabi-
nets, drawers, and even his refrigerator and stove have at one time or
another been called into service as World of Checkers Museum storage

★ ★

and display space. (Not to worry, you little fire marshals in training: Don said he unplugged the stove and refrigerator first.)

And the best part is, his home and museum are open to the public for all to enjoy. "It's like the *Mona Lisa*," Mr. Checkers said of his museum. "You have to really see it to appreciate it." The *Mona Lisa* should be so lucky to have as passionate and single-minded a caretaker (and roommate) as Don Deweber.

If you'd like to visit Don and his World of Checkers Museum, call (563) 556-1944 or e-mail him at checkers21@hotmail.com.

Farmers and Their Toys
Dyersville

If the wisdom on bumper stickers is true, and those with the most toys truly do win, then the National Farm Toy Museum in Dyersville is the winner many times over. With two floors of more than 30,000 farm toys and exhibits, ranging from row after row of common tractors to combines, harvesters, and haulers, all the way down the extensive agricultural machinery lineup to the anhydrous ammonia tanker, the museum is a shrine in miniature to the heavy equipment Iowa farmers fuss over, endlessly fix, periodically live in (during planting and harvesting), and tirelessly operate to bring home the grain or the beans that bring home the bacon.

And don't let the word *toy* fool you—the only thing toylike about these farm toys is that they're built to $\frac{1}{16}$ or $\frac{1}{32}$ scale and don't have internal-combustion engines. This is Iowa, after all, and farm machines aren't child's play, even when they're toys. Most of the toys are stunningly accurate, not to mention beautiful, replicas of tractors or combines from particular makers—like John Deere and Case— from particular years, with details accurate down to the windshield wipers. Children playing with these toys not only got to have fun, they got a vocational education in heavy equipment.

Highlights of the museum include an exhibit explaining the notion of scale that features a full-size replica of a John Deere tractor accompanied by a row of successively smaller scale models, from ½ scale all the way down to a realistic-looking tractor you can carry in your pocket. Upstairs look for more tractors and harvesters enclosed in glass cases—more, perhaps, than you ever hoped to see.

And though the word *toy* does, technically, appear in this museum's name, don't expect much playing around here. Tractors, trucks, trailers, and combines, even at ⅟₃₂ or even ⅟₆₄ scale, are way too wrapped up in Iowa's blood, sweat, and sorrow to be simple objects of play. Don't be surprised if you see some old-timer kicking the tires of a tiny Case Combine, wondering how it would hold up harvesting more than 2,000 acres, or some young 'un quietly cussing a pocket-size John Deere because it won't turn over.

The National Farm Toy Museum is at the intersection of US 20 and IA 136 in Dyersville. Open daily from 8:00 a.m. to 6:00 p.m., the museum also hosts a number of special events and exhibits throughout the year, the largest of which is the "granddaddy of all farm toy shows," held the first full weekend of November. For more information, call (563) 875-2727 or visit www.nationalfarmtoymuseum.com.

Hollywood Dreamin' in Iowa

Dyersville

Even though Iowa has no professional baseball team, over the last twenty years more than a million people from all over the world have come to visit a small ballpark just outside Dyersville.

In 1989 *Field of Dreams* was filmed on the ninety-one-year-old Lansing family farm just outside Dyersville, after the Iowa Film Board pitched it to Hollywood as the perfect spot for a movie about a farmer, Ray Kinsella (played by Kevin Costner), who turns a portion of his acreage into a baseball diamond after hearing a voice and having visions. Sources say the Film Board made their case to the Hollywood execs by saying there were plenty of Iowans who hear voices and have visions all the time. Sure, some Nebraskans hear voices, and

★ ★

The ball field that a hallucinating farmer built. Catherine Cole

some Minnesotans have visions, but Iowa has the highest percentage of hallucinatory farmers. Hollywood was sold.

During filming in the summer of 1988, the house got a new wrap-around porch, and the baseball field, with its Little League–size infield and telephone-pole-style lighting, was built in three days. Once the filming was over, the Lansings—and their neighbor, Al Ameskamp, who happened to own the center- and left-field property—hadn't even had a chance to convert the land back to tillage before tourists started showing up to get a look at the real Field of Dreams. And once the Lansings and the Ameskamps saw that more than 50,000 people a year would visit, with money burning holes in their pockets, it didn't take the neighbors long to start feuding. The end result was a Siamese twin of a tourist attraction, conjoined at the infield but with two competing souvenir stands. The Ameskamps called their site Left & Center Field of Dreams (which doesn't exactly roll off the tongue), peddling their wares along the third-base line, while the Lansings took the name Field of Dreams and set up a souvenir booth at the top of their driveway.

In 2007 the Ameskamps sold out to the Lansings, and the Field of Dreams became a little less schizophrenic. (The two sites had differ- ent closing times, which got a little confusing for visitors.) Whether two sites or one, families keep coming, summer after summer, to play catch, hit a few balls, and see the place where a baseball film was made that captured their hearts.

Dyersville is just off US 20, about 25 miles west of Dubuque. To get to the Field of Dreams, head north out of town on IA 136, cross the railroad tracks, and then take a right onto Third Avenue NE. From there it's about 4 miles to the field; just follow the signs. Open daily April through November, 9:00 a.m. to 6:00 p.m. Call (563) 875-8404 for more information.

Tie a Yellow Ribbon 'round the Old Stone Man
Fayette

Just west of Fayette at a T intersection on a gravel road sits one of the county's most famous residents—the Stone Man. Only 3½ feet tall but weighing an impressive one-half ton, the Stone Man is really a granite boulder vaguely resembling a human (why Stone Man and not Stone Woman, we're not sure), in much the same way a cloud can resemble Richard Nixon's profile. There's a certain rough resem- blance for your imagination to work with, but not a whole lot of verisimilitude.

And therein lies the Stone Man's charm. Sitting in his humble drainage ditch, half-obscured by weeds, he looks like the forgot- ten work of some prehistoric sculptor. Unlike slightly more famous American rock landmarks, like Mount Rushmore, the Stone Man's crude form, tiny size, and utter lack of pretension (just a small plaque identifies him) can make suckers for the underdog like me swoon at

★ ★

his feet, or, more truthfully, his wide, footless, legless base. He's the kind of 3-foot Stone Man who makes you want to take him home and mother him.

Not much is known about the Stone Man, which only adds to his appeal, of course—everyone loves a man of mystery. Where did he come from? What purpose, if any, did he serve? Levern and Jo Ellen Knight, local historians and resident experts on the Stone Man, have done extensive research but have come up with only unsubstantiated theories, the most interesting of which is that the Stone Man served as a boundary marker between early settler and Indian lands. From historical accounts they discovered that the Stone Man has been used as a meeting spot and guidepost for travelers as far back as the 1880s. Settlers would give directions by saying things like, "Drive

A little man who once had a big wardrobe. Catherine Cole

your team past a whole lot of corn, and when you get to the Stone Man, bang a right and you're almost there."

Farm families would often meet at the Stone Man before heading into town for church or shopping, but if one family decided not to wait for the others, they'd tie father's necktie around the Stone Man, or place mother's bonnet on his head as a sign that they'd gone ahead. According to some accounts, the Stone Man sported a different piece of clothing almost every day of summer and therefore appeared to have one of the most extensive wardrobes in the county. And, although we can't ever be certain of this, he was probably one of the only men in the county to regularly sport a church bonnet.

Head north out of Fayette on IA 150 about half a mile to the top of the hill and then take a left onto 152nd Street. Travel west on 152nd for about 2 miles until it ends at M Street. At the intersection look to the left, and you'll see the Stone Man peeking up from the grasses or the snow, depending on the time of year.

Church for Eight (or a Crowded Twelve)
Festina

We might as well get the bitter truth out of the way up front: Though many people claim St. Anthony of Padua Chapel in Festina to be the "World's Smallest Church" (including my Iowa Department of Transportation Map), it is most certainly not. Just to give one example, at 12 by 16 feet, St. Anthony's is significantly larger than the so-called Smallest Church in America in South Newport, Georgia, which measures 10 by 15 feet. And the people way down in Georgia may be excused for never having heard of the much smaller 4-by-6-foot chapel in Oneida, New York, with just enough room for minister, bride, groom, and perhaps one very small flower girl.

Even though the St. Anthony of Padua Chapel has a monstrous (by small church standards) 30-foot steeple, a regular-size door, and comfortable seating for eight to twelve thin Iowans, the chapel somehow still gained some measure of fame as the "World's Smallest

The littlest church on the prairie.

Church." Was it a Festina Chamber of Commerce conspiracy to sup-
press information about smaller chapels worldwide? A case of local
pride winning out against the hard facts? Or just good old-fashioned
hometown boosterism? Whatever the reason, whether innocent or
diabolical, the church is frequently, but usually unofficially, referred to
as the "World's Smallest Church."

Built in 1885 by Mary Ann and Frank Joseph Huber to fulfill a
promise by Mary Ann's grandmother to build a church if her son

returned home safely from war, the chapel contains four robin's-egg-blue pews, four simple stained-glass windows, and a tiny altar with a statue of St. Anthony. Located on quiet, tree-shaded grounds, surrounded by some of the most beautiful farms in the world, the church may not be the smallest around, but it's certainly one of the prettiest.

Thankfully, most official information and signage for the church makes no world-record claims, once again confirming Iowans as more or less trustworthy folk. The small blue signs directing you down gravel roads past rolling green hills and Swiss Valley farms to St. Anthony's say simply LITTLEST CHURCH. Potentially misleading? Yes. A lie? Not really. They're signs a politician could stand behind, and that's good enough for us.

Take 123rd Street west out of Festina about 2 miles, then take a left on Little Church Road (now here's an honest sign—the church is, in fact, little). St. Anthony of Padua Chapel is about 1 mile down the road on the left.

Historic Mounds w/View

Harpers Ferry

To say that European settlers are relative newcomers to Iowa is perhaps a bit of an understatement. Native peoples lived in Iowa for at least 12,000 years before we Johnny-come-latelies started building settler's log cabins about 160 years ago.

But what physical record remains of their 12,000 years here in Iowa? Native peoples weren't into large-scale agribusiness, interstate highways, or permanent dwellings, but in northeastern Iowa they left behind thousands and thousands of mysterious earthen mounds, 3 to 4 feet in height and up to 200 feet long, many of them in the shapes of birds, turtles, lizards, bison, and, most commonly, bears. Most of the mounds, unfortunately, have fallen to the plow over the last century. Surveys in the late-nineteenth and early-twentieth centuries documented more than 10,000 mounds in the region, but by the end of the century, fewer than 1,000 remained.

★ ★

Of those surviving mounds, 195 are located in Effigy Mounds National Monument, a beautiful 2,526-acre park located just north of Marquette along the banks of the Mississippi. Dating from between 3,000 and 750 years ago, the mounds are one of the only records we have of the people who once flourished along the river, fishing,

Guess What? Another Ringer!

There are lots of ways to make it into the *Guinness Book of World Records* (see, for example, "Popcorn Ball for 6,000?" in chapter 5), but Glen "Red" Henton of Maquoketa did it the old-fashioned way: He earned it.

How, you ask? By pitching more ringers in a single World Tournament horseshoes match than any other player in history. In that epic 1965 game against Ray Martin in Keene, New Hampshire, a match Guinness certified as the "Greatest Horseshoe Game Ever," Red pitched a world-record 175 ringers and another world-record total 80 double ringers. Together he and Ray pitched a grand total of 388 horseshoes during their two-and-a-half-hour exhibition of superhuman concentration, and 349 of those tosses, or just a hair shy of 90 percent of them, were perfect ringers. To put the game in perspective, that's like two pro basketball players facing off against each other in a two-and-a-half-hour free-throw contest to decide the NBA championship, and then both hitting nine out of every ten shots. During their match, all four shoes were on the stake an unbelievable sixty-three times.

To say Red and Ray were on fire would be an understatement: More

hunting white-tailed deer, and harvesting freshwater mussels, wild rice, acorns, and berries.

The majority of the mounds are conical or linear in shape, but thirty-two of them take the form of animal effigies. At Effigy, you'll find earthen mounds in the shape of both birds and bears; one bird

accurately, they both decided to go nuclear during the same match. Together the pair still holds single-game world records for longest game, most total ringers, most double ringers, most canceled ringers, and most "four deads," a rather somber-sounding term for the impressive feat of landing all four horseshoes around the stake.

And what was Red's response to my questions about that magical game? "I did alright," he said. Now that's a man who's humble beyond reason. He probably thinks it's pretty okay that he won nineteen state titles over the course of his career and in 1978 was inducted into the National Horseshoe Pitching Hall of Fame. "I was just relaxed and throwing ringers that game," he told me. "You need to have very deep concentration. When I got focused in, you could have shot a cannon off and I wouldn't have noticed. And if he hit a ringer, well, that's fine. And if my shoe hit the stake and then bounced off, that's fine too. You just have to stay focused." And if you happen to pitch the world's greatest game of horseshoes ever, well, that's not too bad a day's work either.

Red celebrated his eighty-ninth birthday in 2009 and lives in Maquoketa. He still puts on "shows" for folks who want him to bring his stakes and shoes so they can play some just-for-fun horseshoes with him. Participants need not be ringers, of course. Red's seen plenty of those for one lifetime.

mound at the site has a wingspan of 212 feet, whereas the Great Bear mound is 137 feet long. Though these native inhabitants buried their dead in the conical mounds, experts aren't sure what purpose the animal-shaped mounds served, and with no written records and few surviving tribal stories, the role of the mounds in this culture is likely to remain a mystery.

A 2- or 3-mile hike through forests of oak, maple, shagbark hickory, and birch takes you past numerous animal mounds to lookout spots atop 350-foot-high bluffs with names like Hanging Rock and Fire Point, where you can take in some of the most breathtaking views of the Mississippi anywhere along its banks. Whatever the purpose of the mounds, one thing is certain: The people who built them chose prime real estate upon which to sculpt, basket load by basket load of earth, these bears and birds.

To get to Effigy Mounds, take IA 76 north of Marquette about 3 miles. The visitor center will be on the right. Guided tours are available Memorial Day through Labor Day. For days and hours of operation, call (563) 873-3491 or visit www.nps.gov/efmo.

CAUTION: Large Wake—Elephant Water-Skiing

Marquette

Pinky, a life-size fiberglass pink elephant, used to spend her time greeting patrons in front of the appropriately named but now defunct Pink Elephant Supper Club. Now she stands watch on IA 76 in downtown Marquette, right in front of the casino, her long snout resting no more than 2 or 3 feet from passing traffic. The 14-foot-tall, bleary-eyed behemoth sports formal attire (a slightly askew top hat rests on her head) in order to properly welcome visitors to the Mississippi's first state-licensed gambling facility, the Miss Marquette Riverboat Casino, a barge done up in riverboat style.

Though currently a casino-industry employee, Pinky's crowning moment of glory came in August 1978, when her owner somehow

If you think Pinky looks good now, just picture her in a wet suit. Catherine Cole

coaxed her to water-ski the Mississippi at Prairie du Chien in honor of the visiting Jimmy Carter. Was she hoping President Carter would take her on the road or just take her home to the peanut farm? Whatever motivated Pinky, it seems her hopes for more lasting glory were dashed. (Have you ever seen a pink elephant with such sad eyes?) And since her salad days, she seems to have lost her skis, her bathing suit, and her girlish figure. Here's hoping Pinky returns to the river one day, if not to water-ski, then at least to do a little tubing.

Pinky stands watch in front of the Miss Marquette Riverboat Casino on IA 76 in downtown Marquette.

★ ★

Birthplace of the Greatest Show on Earth
McGregor

Even in a region filled with charming Mississippi River towns, from Bellevue to Guttenberg to North Buena Vista, the small town of McGregor, located just south of Marquette, is a standout. Main Street, sprinkled liberally with cafes, bookstores, inns, and antiques shops, has somehow managed to maintain its authenticity; even on days when it's crowded with out-of-towners like us, McGregor still feels like a real town rather than some tourism-dollars-obsessed reproduction of what it once was.

One of McGregor's main claims to fame is that from 1860 to 1872 it was home to August and Marie Salome Ringling and their seven boys, Albert, August (or A. G.), Otto, Alfred, Charles, John, and Henry. The boys saw their first circuses at the end of Main Street by the riverboat landing, and it wasn't long before they began putting on their own shows, raising a tent themselves in a backyard and charging a penny admission. According to one eyewitness account, the performers numbered only three, two of whom offered suspiciously similar parallel-bar acts for the crowd's amusement. The only animal, exotic or otherwise, was the town horse.

After raising money by giving exhibitions in halls and small-town theaters, five of the Ringling brothers managed to save enough cash to put on their first real circus in the spring of 1884 in Baraboo, Wisconsin. The show required just nine wagons and featured no giraffes; no lions, tigers, or bears; and not a single elephant. By 1907 the Ringling brothers bought out Barnum and Bailey, and by 1929, with the purchase of the American Circus Company for $2 million, John Ringling, the last surviving brother, owned all major circus railroad shows (and a fair number of the gainfully employed elephants) in the United States.

When asked the keys to the Ringling brothers' success, brother Charles is reported to have said, "Hard work, honesty, and a keen sense of what people want." Perhaps that keen ability to know what

★ ★

people really want is what made the boys drop the dual parallel-bar acts and pick up some giraffes, a few leotard-clad trapeze artists, and a bunch of ferocious tigers willing to jump through flaming hoops. Pure genius.

In McGregor you can visit the former Ringling home, just a few blocks from the end of Main Street, and see where this greatest of circus dynasties began. Follow Main Street away from the river until the T intersection at Seventh Street. Take a left onto Seventh and then a right on Walton Street. The former Ringling home is at 61 Walton Street. Look for the small historical marker out front. For more information, contact the McGregor Historical Museum at (563) 873-2221.

For the Love of Chain-Saw Art
McGregor

There are some people, like chain-saw artist Dan Slaughter, who are lucky enough to find their true passion in life by chance one day and then never look back. For years he ran an auto-body shop out of his garage until one fateful day when a friend asked him if he could fix his electric chain saw. "Well, I replaced the cord and then I went out back to see if it would work," he told me. "I set up a log between two sawhorses and I got the chain saw runnin', and for some reason I started cutting a bear out of the log. And it looked pretty good." ("But why do you think you just started carving?" I pressed him a couple of times, but he couldn't say.) "The next day I took my body-shop sign down, finished the two or three cars I had left, and never looked back."

Well, it wasn't actually quite that simple: He had to check with his wife first. But after the missus gave him the okay to quit his paying job and start chain-saw-carving things like the Tin Man and Mr. Peanut and really anything else that suits his fancy full-time, Dan felt, he said, "a real peace of mind." I didn't have the heart to ask him if the same could be said of Mrs. Slaughter.

Now Dan's yard is chockablock full of his chain-saw handiwork, with totem-pole-style representations of everything from Elvis to Betty Boop to space aliens to Uncle Sam. I assumed they were for sale, but that's not exactly the case. "I like them all pretty well," he told me, "so I don't really want to see them go. But if someone really likes something and then goes home and can't sleep at night cause they're thinking about it, well then I'll let them have it." Not exactly a recipe for banner sales, but, sensibly enough, Dan's not in the chain-saw art business for the money. "I don't do anything [artwork] for nobody. You know, if someone wants a carving of something from me, I won't do it. You understand what I'm handin' ya? That would make it too commercial, and I don't like that."

What does he like? He really enjoys heading out to his yard to work on whatever piques his curiosity that day. And he likes having visitors stop in and check out his huge collection of sculptures, old signs, and antiques. He'll offer a cup of coffee and, if you'd like something to eat along with it, then a cookie, too, and he'll sit on the patio and chew the fat. Best to come in the afternoon, though—"I'm no good in the mornings," he told me without apology. And if you absolutely must have some quirky creation you see in his yard, he'll be mostly happy to oblige.

Dan Slaughter's place is located at 30279 Klein Brewery Road (IA 18), about 1 mile west of McGregor. His phone number is (319) 873-3711.

A Wooden-Chain-Lover's Paradise
Monona

Small-town historical museums in Iowa are odd mixtures, one part antiques store (where the items are not for sale), one part communal attic of strange keepsakes, and one part local celebrity show. For example, though the Monona Historical Museum contains the obligatory antique barber's chair, old refrigerator, and even older stove (all in excellent shape), it also has on display the First Monona Telephone

Link by link, just take it link by link.

Switchboard; a fair amount of Monona High School memorabilia, including old band uniforms and jerseys; various scary-looking items from the old area hospital; and a whole lot of hand-carved wooden chains.

★ ★

For all the excitement of pulling on the switchboard cords and placing imaginary calls (it really was kind of exciting), the Monona Historical Museum's most fascinating items, of course, are the rows and rows of hand-carved wooden chains. With more than 400 chains on display in an addition built solely to house the carvings, the collection is quite honestly (and safely) hailed as the "World's Largest Known Collection of Hand Carved Chains." In other words, if there's a bigger collection out there, the museum board members sure haven't heard of it.

Local Elmer Marting Sr. began carving the chains after retiring from farming and discovering (to his dismay, we must imagine) that he didn't enjoy fishing or playing cards. What else to do, then, but carve hundreds upon hundreds of wooden chains? Elmer ended up spending a fair amount of his retirement painstakingly crafting chains from single pieces of wood using no glue, only simple carving tools and a tireless imagination for coming up with infinite variations on a theme. There are straight chains and twisted chains and chains composed of box-shaped links, some with wooden balls inside; there are teak chains and cypress chains, ironwood and burly pecan chains, coco bolo, and mulberry; there are chains carved from broom handles, from pencils (for writing chain letters, Elmer liked to say), and, miraculously, from a standard round toothpick. There's even an American flag made of wooden chains, one chain for each stripe.

Looking at all these chains, it's easy to forget that each one represents weeks of painstaking work. Though Elmer enjoyed showing the chains at county fairs, he didn't sell that many, simply because the many hours of work required to make each chain made them prohibitively expensive to buy. And he wasn't that interested in selling them to begin with, in part due to some shrewd thinking. Carol Marting, Elmer's daughter-in-law and one of the museum's tour guides, said that one reason Elmer donated the whole collection to the museum (after giving relatives a select few chains) was to prevent someone from selling it. "He used to say, 'If you sell them, you've got money, and when you've got money, you spend it, and after you spend it, you've got nothing.'" And 400 hand-carved chains in the hand (or hanging along four museum walls), each with its own variations and charms, are far better than nothing.

Located at 304 South Egbert Street, across the street from Monona City Park, the museum is open Monday through Friday from 1:00 to 4:00 p.m. and weekends by appointment. Call (563) 539-2640 to schedule a visit, or you can visit www.mononahistorical museum.org.

The Church Built by (but not for) a Song
Nashua

Find a beautiful old church in an idyllic country setting, and you can be sure people will line up months ahead of time to get hitched there. Throw a little churchly fame into the deal, though, and you've got a marriage business that might make a cash-strapped minister turn green with envy. Nashua's famous Little Brown Church in the Vale meets these criteria perfectly, and, if its annual wedding reunion the first Sunday in August—attended by as many as 500 people—is any indication, the place sees as many marriages as a roadside Vegas chapel.

The church's fame is attributable to William Pitts and the four Weather-wax brothers. (Sounds like a country music act, doesn't it?) Pitts was a young music teacher who, on his way to visit his girlfriend in June of 1857, made a stagecoach pit stop beside what would one day become the Little Brown Church grounds. Moved by the beauty of the spot, the gently rolling hills, the creek, the ancient evergreens and hardwoods, he imagined how lovely a country church would look there. (Wonder why his mind was on churches. High hopes?) Upon returning home to southern Wisconsin after his visit, he wrote a poem about his imagined church, set it to music, and titled it "The Church in the Wildwood."

Years passed, and when Pitts eventually returned to the area to teach music, he was shocked to see that a church was being built

★ ★

in the very spot he'd imagined. His Bradford Academy vocal class sang the lines, "There's a church in the valley by the wild-wood / No lovelier spot in the dale / No place is so dear to my childhood / As the little brown church in the vale," in public for the first time at the church's dedication in 1864. No sentimentalist, Pitts then sold the song to a Chicago publisher for $25 to help finance a medical education in Chicago, but it wasn't until decades later that the Weatherwax brothers, a popular gospel quartet from Charles City, made the

You'll find the Little Brown Church in the Weeds just behind the Little Brown Church in the Vale. Catherine Cole

song famous by telling Pitts's story and performing "The Church in the Wildwood" at the end of every show.

The Little Brown Church is now an interesting mix of the religious, the secular, and the commercial. Pictures of Abraham Lincoln and George Washington hang on the church walls; plastic lawn ornaments sprout from the flower beds out front; and a hotel, restaurant, and souvenir shop sit just a stone's throw away from the church's front door. (Be sure to check out the mini replica of the church by the restrooms located right behind the real church.) The grounds are quite breathtaking and the church is beautiful, but you don't have to look hard to find a little Vegas here, too.

Since 1952 the Little Brown Church has hosted its annual wedding reunion the first Sunday in August. Though it's geared toward couples who have married at the church, the celebration is open to all. The highlight of the event is the Service of Recommitment of the Wedding Vows, wherein couples renew their pledges of lifelong love and fidelity. One visitor, a divorcé who wished to remain anonymous, suggested that the Little Brown Church hold another yearly celebration, a sort of singles party in the vale for people who didn't get it right the first time and hope to give the Little Brown Church one, or maybe even two, more tries.

The Little Brown Church is located 2 miles east of Nashua on IA 346. The church is open from early morning to evening every day, and worship service is offered each Sunday at 10:30 a.m. For more information, call (641) 435-2027.

Dying for a Well-Built Coffin?
Peosta

According to casket-business lingo, there are only two kinds of customers: "pre-need" and "need." If you're stumped as to which category you belong, just have a friend or loved one check for a pulse; if there's a heartbeat, then you're a "pre-need" casket shopper, and if not, well, you really need one, right now. (In fact, a casket, some

★ ★

heavy makeup, and a nice suit of clothes are the only things you'll need for a long, long time.)

Pre-need or need, you still want to get the best deal on your eternal digs, and the monks at New Melleray Abbey, located about 12 miles southwest of Dubuque, can help. Whereas most Trappists prefer making jellies and jams to keep their monasteries afloat, the brothers at this towering limestone abbey on a hill selectively harvest trees from

Keep Your Eye on the Corn

In Iowa, sitting and watching the corn grow has to be one of the three most popular summer pastimes, just behind eating corn (number 2) and selling corn from the back of a pickup on the side of the road (number 1). For all those people unlucky enough to be living out of "ear-sight" in the summer, though, either because they live in town or happen to be from someplace else, like Boise or Tulsa or the Bronx, *Iowa Farmer Today*, a Cedar Rapids–based agriculture publication, offers the consolation of CornCam.

CornCam casts an international spotlight on Brad and Kelly Buchanan's 200-acre farm between Cedar Rapids and Ely, offering daily updated images of the corn throughout the spring, summer, and early fall. In the prime growing months of June and July, the Web site can log as many as 40,000 visits from corn lovers all over the country and all over the world. As of this writing, the CornCam shows a pleasant view of tall stalks and arching golden tassels under a nearly cloudless sky of blue. Looking at the picture, it's hard not to feel that all is well on this little patch of earth.

their 3,400-acre farm, mill the lumber themselves, and then use it to craft beautifully austere and downright affordable coffins. Their Simple Rectangular Casket model in pine or oak and lined in muslin (no gaudy satin here) sells for $975, while their top-of-the-line Premium Rectangular Caskets, in walnut or oak, top out at about $2,600.

Founded by Irish monks in 1849, New Melleray was once home to as many as 150 Trappists, but the population is now down to about

Bob Davis, online director for *Iowa Farmer Today*, doesn't fully understand why the site is so popular, but he thinks it has something to do with the fact that corn registers pretty high on the romantic-vegetable scale. And he has some statistics to back up his theory: When *Iowa Farmer Today* ran a SoybeanCam for two years (we're not joking here), it received 90 percent less traffic than CornCam. "The romance wasn't there as it is for corn," Bob said.

In addition to the CornCam, the *Iowa Farmer Today* Web site offers such links as "A Corn Grower's Guidebook," "A Look at the Kernel," and "The Corn Rootworm Homepage," where you can learn everything you wanted to know, and then some, about the surprisingly complex business of growing corn. You can also e-mail the CornCam Web site and let them know your thoughts or even ask a question. One enthusiastic respondent gave the site a ringing endorsement: "If there's a better site for watching corn grow," he wrote, "I haven't seen it." And another visitor asked a seemingly unanswerable question: "Why is this site so exciting?" As Iowans, we'll naturally assume the question is rhetorical.

To sit and watch the corn grow, go to www.iowafarmer.com/corn_cam.

Iowa
CURIOSITIES

★ ★

30 monks. A Roman Catholic order that originated in La Trappe, France, in the mid-seventeenth century, the Trappists follow the monastic rule of St. Benedict, which consists of contemplative prayer, community worship, and manual labor. For the New Melleray monks, that means rising at 3:15 a.m. each morning for prayer, attending church services seven times a day, refraining from eating meat, and working four or five hours each day, either in one of the abbey's fields of soy, corn, alfalfa, or potatoes, or turning out simple caskets for both pre-need and in-desperate-need customers.

New Melleray Abbey is located south of Peosta at 6500 Melleray Circle, midway between US 151 and US 20. They offer simple accommodations and meals for visitors wishing to spend time at the monastery, either as monastic retreatants or simply as guests. (A free-will offering of $30 per day is suggested.) For more information, call (563) 588-2319. To order a casket, call (888) 433-6934 or visit www.trappistcasket.com.

The Glory of Being Grump for a Year
Readlyn

Readlyn posts a warning for all to see on a sign located at the edge of town. READLYN, the sign reads, HOME TO 857 FRIENDLY PEOPLE & ONE OLD GRUMP. Depending on how many grumps you have in your neighborhood (or in your own family), you may think this quite a remarkable nice-person-to-grump ratio, but remember, this is Iowa, where nice people are almost as plentiful as hogs.

So who's the old grump, you wonder? Does he live on the wrong side of the tracks in a tiny shack, hurling insults at the merry mailman, the good-natured garbage collector, the pious paperboy? The sign, however, is a little dishonest on two counts: First, there are actually about ten grumps in town, all over the age of sixty-five, and second, all of them are, according to local Jackie Clemmens, "just the opposite of grumpy."

★ ★

Don't say the people of Readlyn didn't warn you.

Back in 1990 the Readlyn Community Club came up with the idea of electing a town grump every year on the third weekend in June and then holding a Grump Fest in his or her honor. Though you might imagine the qualifications to run for Readlyn grump are quite strict—say, at least ten years of complaining bitterly about present-day youth and fifteen years of telling stories about how things were so much tougher in the old days—the only two qualifications necessary are (1) the prospective grump must live in Readlyn, and (2) he or she must be sixty-five or older.

With such minimal qualifications, it's no wonder the Community Club has managed to select the sorriest bunch of grumps you'll ever meet. As far as we know, not a single one of the so-called grumps has ever cussed a neighborhood dog, turned off the lights and hid on Halloween, or sneered at the thought of a good, old-fashioned hometown parade. On the contrary, each year the town grump

★ ★

marches in the Grump Fest parade, right beside the year's Miss Read-lyn, a local high school senior, smiling away in a most ungrumplike fashion. And, each year, Readlyn's grump attends local events and celebrations, marches in county parades, speaks with both the local and national media, and generally serves as an all-too-good-natured Readlyn town ambassador. It's enough to make you long for some good old-fashioned surliness.

If you're really searching for some ill will, Readlyn's annual Grump Fest will be a big disappointment, unless, of course, the beer tent happens to run out of Bud. Highlights of the Grump Fest include dancing; not one, but two card tournaments (Shuffscup and Pepper); a local talent show where everyone gets a lot of applause, no matter the level of talent; and, of course, a parade featuring the newly coro-nated grump as well as all past surviving grumps.

So, if you go, be sure to be on your best behavior, and don't, we repeat, don't heckle the accordion player at the talent show. If you do, not even the town grumps will think you're funny.

Readlyn is located just south of IA 3 on CR V49, midway between Waverly and Oelwein. Grump Fest is held the third weekend of June. For more information, call the city clerk's office at (319) 279-3411.

Former Fast-Food Poster Boy Finds Work as Umpire
Ryan

It's not easy starting a whole new career in middle age, especially if you happen to be an inflexible 20-foot-tall fiberglass Happy Chef. But with the help of a flatbed truck, about twenty-five strong friends, and a creative auto-body worker, even a statue who's spent his entire life wearing a chef's hat and peddling fast food can find a new home and gainful employment to boot, in this case as an intimidatingly large home-plate ump.

Ryan's town park is home to "Iowa's Largest Umpire Statue" (seems like a rather conservative claim, doesn't it?), a former Happy Chef statue from Cedar Rapids that would have been doomed to

A new career at the ballpark for a lifelong fast-food industry poster boy. Will Jennings

the large fiberglass statuary dustheap if it hadn't been for the inter-cession of a local priest, Father Beelner. According to postmaster Leo Wood, one of the men who helped the Happy Chef through his career transition, Father Beelner had long wanted "something

★ ★

distinguished for the park—you know, a tank or a jet or something," so when local Pat McKelly's Cedar Rapids Happy Chef franchise was getting rid of their mascot for a new and improved look, he knew whom to call. "Pat called Father Beelner up and he said, 'If you want something for that ballpark, we're getting rid of our Happy Chef. If you want him, you better come and pick him up.'"

And that's just what Father Beelner and a group of local men did. It took more than twenty of them to lift the, at that point, not-so-happy chef by hand (the fiberglass groaned and threatened to break under the strain) onto a flatbed truck and prop it up with hay bales for the 30-mile drive to Ryan. "And at that point we didn't even know what we were going to do with it—we just had a Happy Chef," Wood said. But thanks to the ingenuity of a local auto-body worker, the chef became an umpire. "Jerry did a great job: He took his hat off, put his thumb up, gave him a mask . . . and did you see the paint job on him?" He now stands watch over Ryan's ballpark, his thumb raised in the air, calling everybody out in a genial way alto-gether uncharacteristic for an ump—with a nice big smile. It seems once a Happy Chef, always a Happy Chef, or at least always happy, even when dressed up in an ump's clothes and giving everybody the heave-ho.

Ryan is located on IA 13, 8 miles south of US 20. The umpire stands at the corner of Ryan Park, just behind the baseball diamond.

Bully for Bily Clocks
Spillville

What's a couple of bachelor Bohemian brother farmers named Bily (pronounced *bee-lee*) to do during the long, cold northeastern Iowa winters, especially with no wives or children or mothers-in-law to keep them otherwise occupied? Should they (a) take up quilting and sell their handiwork at the county fair; (b) become ham-radio enthu-siasts and try to communicate with old acquaintances in their Czech homeland; (c) take up wood carving and painstakingly build some of the biggest and most intricate clocks you've ever seen; (d) take to the bottle, sleep 'til noon, and give up showering; or (e) all of the above?

If you said "e," congratulations, you've got a twisted imagination, but if you wisely answered "c," you're absolutely correct. Brothers Frank and Joseph Bily carved their Bily Clocks every winter for more than forty-five years, in spite of their father's advice that they would be far better off if they spent their time doing something more practical.

But what clocks they are! All of the main timepieces are big (8 or 9 feet tall) and elaborately, no, obsessively carved, covered with minutely detailed architectural-style features such as columns, balustrades, and cornices, as well as carved mechanical figures, including saints, apostles, cuckoos, and prominent figures from American history. And, to top it all off, many contain built-in musical chimes. The most elaborate of the clocks took years to build, and each one stands as testament to the skill and dedication of these two brothers who never traveled more than 35 miles from Spillville, as well as to the mind-numbing boredom of Iowa winters early in the twentieth century.

Highlights of the collection, housed in an old brick-front residence in downtown Spillville, include the Apostle Clock (built 1915–16), which disgorges twelve wooden apostles in a tight-knit group every hour on the hour; the American Pioneer History Clock (1923–27), which stands 8 feet tall, weighs more than 500 pounds, and contains fifty-seven panels, each one highlighting an important event in U.S. history; and the Charles Lindbergh Memorial Clock (1928), featuring a carved portrait of Lindbergh in honor of his heroic flight.

The Bily Clock Museum also contains a second floor exhibit honoring the famous Czech composer Antonín Dvořák, who lived in the home with his family during the summer of 1893. Though it's not known for certain whether Frank and Joseph ever met Dvořák (they were only boys at the time of his visit), they made a clock in his memory, anyway; it's in the shape of a violin with Dvořák's face, bushy

★ ★

beard and all, carved into the body. And why not honor the composer with a clock? After all, the Iowa winters are long, the brothers sure as heck weren't going anywhere, and a couple of carvers probably start to run thin on subjects after forty years of clock making.

The Bily Clock Museum is located at 323 North Main Street, downtown Spillville. May through October the museum is open Monday through Saturday from 9:00 a.m. to 5:00 p.m. and Sunday noon to 4:00 p.m. In April and November the museum's only open on weekends, with hours from 10:00 a.m. to 4:00 p.m. on Saturday and noon to 4:00 p.m. on Sunday. The museum is closed December through March, perhaps in honor of Frank and Joseph's prime clock-building season. For more information, call (563) 562-3569 or visit www.bilyclocks.org.

World's Largest Fiberglass Strawberry on a Pole
Strawberry Point

Strawberries aren't very hard to find in this town, at least on signs. Like an egomaniacal parent, the delicate little fruit seems to have given its name to just about every hotel, gift shop, and gathering in town. Just to give a few examples, lest we belabor the point, Strawberry Point is home to the Strawberry Motel, Strawberry Computing, Strawberry Foods, Deli & Bakery, and even Strawberry Leisure Homes.

Actually, we can't blame the strawberry for the proliferation of its moniker in Strawberry Point, but we can blame the Frank Hardy Ad Agency in Dubuque and the tourism-savvy Strawberry Point citizens who dreamt up a 15-foot-tall fiberglass strawberry, complete with glistening yellow seeds, and perched it atop a pole smack dab in front of City Hall. The Strawberry Point strawberry was manufactured in California—where else would the world's biggest strawberry come from?—and then traveled cross-country by train before its installation on June 20, 1967. Towering 29 feet above Main Street and hailed as "The Largest Strawberry in the World," the sculpture immediately became a tourist attraction and helped encourage the de facto policy

A big berry that spread its name all over town.

of naming everything in town "Strawberry," from the motel to the leisure home outfit.

Harry Nolda, owner of Strawberry Point's *Press Journal,* was one of the people instrumental in bringing the world's biggest strawberry to town. "We just were sitting around, and I can't remember who came up with the idea. At first we thought it was kind of crazy, but then we said, 'Why not?' And so we did it." (Don't most stories, both tragic and comic, begin just that way?) The Jaycees went door to door collecting money from townspeople, raising more than

$4,300 of the strawberry's $6,700 cost. The town chipped in the rest. Though the group had hoped to deliver the strawberry to City Hall by helicopter ("It would have been something," Harry said, "a 15-foot-tall strawberry dangling from a helicopter.") the cost was prohibitively high, so it rolled in from Dubuque by truck.

With the name and the big statue, you might imagine Strawberry Point grows lots of strawberries, but you'd be wrong. (I was told not to say so, but I'm terrible at keeping secrets: They don't really grow any!) The name Strawberry Point came from nineteenth-century soldiers who made frequent stops at a spring outside town where wild strawberries grew, a spot they called Strawberry Point, on their way between Dubuque and Fort Atkinson. Now, the town celebrates its heritage with a Strawberry Days Festival, featuring tractor pulls, barbershop quartets, and loads of free—yes, that's right, free—strawberries and ice cream.

Here's hoping that the giant strawberry stands tall over Strawberry Point for many years to come, and here's hoping, too, that one day it loosens its death grip on the imaginations of the town's small-business owners. In the meantime, if you're looking for a florist, a Laundromat, a baker, or maybe even a mortician in town, just look in the phone book under "strawberry."

Strawberry Point is located due east of Oelwein, at the intersection of IA 3 and IA 13. The world's largest strawberry can be found downtown, right in front of City Hall. The Strawberry Days Festival is held each summer in the middle of June, with free strawberries and ice cream served at the firehouse on Sunday. Call Fay Falck at (563) 933-4370 for more information.

Even Honest Abe Wrestled
Waterloo

According to Mike Chapman, executive director of Waterloo's Dan Gable International Wrestling Institute and Museum, Frank Gotch was the man who sparked Iowa's love affair with wrestling. He also happens to be Mike's hero as well.

At the turn of the twentieth century, professional wrestling was a legitimate sport that drew large crowds, and George "the Russian Lion" Hackenschmidt was the undisputed champion of the world. And then Iowa's own Frank Gotch came along. On April 3, 1908, Gotch defeated Hackenschmidt in a match that lasted two hours and three minutes. Iowans were swept up in Gotch-mania. Thousands of young boys read dramatic stories about their home-state hero and dreamt of being just like Frank—Iowa had become a wrestling state. When a rematch was held on September 4, 1911, at Chicago's Comiskey Park in front of a crowd of 33,000 and Gotch once again defeated the Russian Lion, his status as a legendary Iowan was affirmed.

You can find a full Gotch exhibit at the Wrestling Institute and Museum, along with displays on more contemporary Iowa wrestling legends, exhibits on wrestling in antiquity, hundreds of plaques featuring the names of every NCAA wrestling champ in every weight class for the last forty or fifty years, and all sorts of other grappling memorabilia. Fans of Dan Gable—four-time NCAA championship wrestler at the University of Iowa, 1972 Olympic champion who didn't lose a single Olympic point (the wrestling equivalent of winning Wimbledon without dropping a single game), and University of Iowa coach who won fifteen titles and earned a 131–2 Big Ten record—will find everything from childhood photographs and old newspaper articles to the scale at West Waterloo High on which wrestlers, including Gable, used to weigh in. For someone from out of state, it would be almost impossible to understand Iowa's passion for wrestling, and for Gable, without a visit to the Dan Gable International Wrestling Institute and Museum.

One favorite highlight of mine is a painting of Abe Lincoln wrestling a man named Jack Armstrong, a reputed "village toughie," on a summer day in 1831. The match was reportedly a close one, and though no one knows for sure who came away the victor, Honest Abe looks very threatening, and very much on top of his game, in the

painting. For some reason, though, he's not wearing ear protectors or a singlet. Get that boy some real equipment, and he could have been a contender. He could have been somebody. Maybe, if he was born fifty years later, he could have even wrestled for the Hawks.

The Dan Gable International Wrestling Institute and Museum is located at 303 Jefferson Street, Waterloo. For hours of operation and other information, call (319) 233-0745 or visit www.wrestling museum.org.

More Than 1,000 Clocks That (Thankfully) Don't Chime All at Once
Waukon

Sweeney's House of Clocks & Museum is one of those Iowa wayside treasure troves that doesn't have regular hours, which makes a visit there all the more personal and all the more wonderfully surreal. In order to get into the building, really just an oversize aluminum storage barn, you have to stop at Sweeney's Village Farm and Home Store, the place with the 20-foot-tall fiberglass steer out front, pawing the ground right beside the 30-foot cowboy, who looks suspiciously like a muffler man who's been given a ten-gallon hat and a new paint job.

Ask about the museum at the counter, and a member of one generation or another of the Sweeney family will probably call Norris Shefelbrin to see if he can come down from the retirement community up the hill to open the place up. "They serve dinner to the residents about eleven, eleven-thirty, so he may need to make it quick," one of the Sweeneys told us. The pressure was on.

Norris met us at the door a few minutes later, shook our hands, unlocked the doors, collected his four bucks, and then told us that the oldest clock of the 1,000 or so in the place, made in 1692, was the small black table clock in the back corner. And then, without further ado, he let us know his work was done. "That's about all I can tell you. I just do this as a pastime. And I don't go around and wind

✳ ✳

Does anyone have the time . . . to wind all these clocks?

'em all, either." With that short but refreshingly frank introduction,
he turned us loose to marvel at the rows and rows of mantel clocks,
kitchen clocks, grandfather clocks, and so on, as well as the oddball
assortment of antiques, memorabilia, and artifacts.

Sweeney's House of Clocks and Museum is actually two collections
combined into one. The first is Ray Tlougan's mammoth collection of
clocks, begun in the summer of 1960 when Ray rescued a grandfather clock from a garbage truck and expanded continuously for the
next seventeen years. Restoring the grandfather prompted him to
begin snapping up other damaged clocks, replacing their clockworks,
and repairing their cabinetry. Soon he was not only restoring clocks
but carving his own (more than 75 percent of the collection Ray
made himself), using only a cheap jigsaw and a pocket knife.

Though most of the collection is composed of pretty standard-
looking clocks, there are a few standouts, including a French onyx

★ ★

clock made for an Egyptian ruler in 1878 and a 10-foot-tall Belgian grandfather clock made in the early eighteenth century, featuring a carved stag's head with a full set of antlers at the very top.

The second part of the collection is Ray Sweeney's museum, an eclectic assortment of old stuff, most of which hails from Allamakee County, including a two-cylinder, chain-driven 1907 Sears & Roebuck automobile (in working condition); a chair whose arms, feet, and back are all made of animal horns; two seated, life-size Indians flanked by two mannequins dressed in World War II–era military uniforms; various and sundry political buttons; old china; and a miniature reproduction of Festina's "Littlest Church." In addition to the fascinating sundries inside, Sweeney also dragged six railroad cars, a very small chapel, his boyhood schoolhouse (really), and a restored settler's cabin up the hill, which, needless to say, produces an interesting architectural landscape effect, a mixture of abandoned railroad yard and abandoned historic village.

Norris wasn't quite being honest when he claimed he didn't know anything else about the museum; he ending up pointing out a number of his favorite items, which included the old jalopy and the miniature Festina chapel, and then chewed the fat with us about nothing in particular. And he didn't even rush us the least bit, even though his dinner was surely getting cold.

Sweeney's House of Clocks and Museum is located a half mile south of Waukon on IA 9 and IA 76. Open by appointment only; stop by Sweeney's Village Farm and Home Store or call (563) 568-4577.

2

Southeast

The Southeast is *home to easily the two most unusual towns in the state: Fairfield and Maharishi Vedic City. Vedic City is still young and really more like a subdivision than a city, but they've got a world-class Ayurvedic spa and a one-and-a-half acre Vedic Observatory that looks like a cross between Stonehenge and a huge science fair project. Fairfield's possibly one of the only places in meat-packing-centric Iowa where you'll feel right at home if you're a vegan—it's got more vegetarian eateries than most Iowa towns its size have restaurants. And if you're into Transcendental Meditation and yogic flying, all the better.*

If vegetarian food's not your thing, then check out the Honey Hole Diner with Bait & Tackle Shop in Wapello. They don't serve minnows, but you sure can get them to go.

For great sights, check out Bob Utter's graffiti barn in Columbus Junction, and then drive by a week later and see if you still recognize it. Who knew so many young people would be willing to paint a barn for free? And if you have the time, be sure to stop in at the Johnny Clock Museum in Lockridge. They're not like any clocks you've ever seen before, and Johnny and his wife Pat are wonderful hosts.

For an old-style river town experience, you can't beat Bentonsport. Call ahead to the Greef General Store to make sure Tony will be in town so you can check out his Museum of Artifacts, Wood, and Horns. He doesn't have a phone, but he's got arrowheads and inlaid-wood display cases to spare.

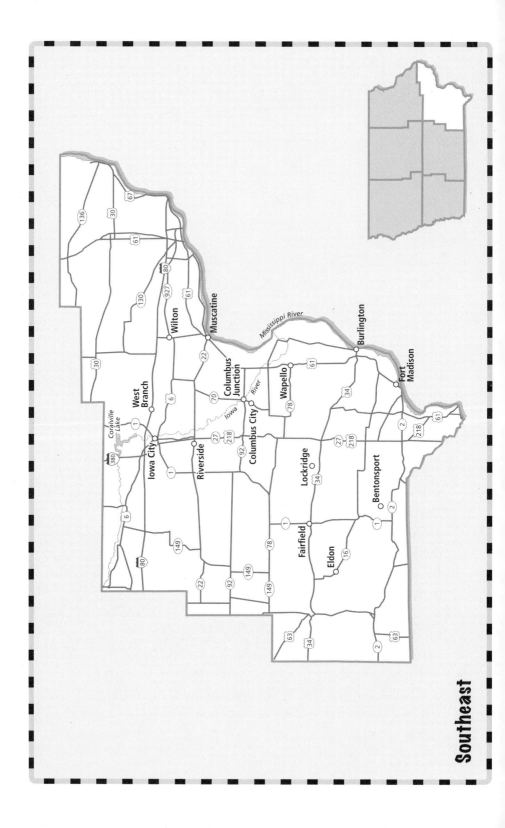

Southeast

★ ★

A Tub for the Exhibitionist in You

Bentonsport

A cross between a living museum and a town, Bentonsport is the most beautiful of the Van Buren County river towns, a tiny place of about 50 residents that was once a bustling steamboat port and home to more than 1,500. Many of the buildings, most of which date from the mid-nineteenth century, have white placards out front listing the date of construction and a brief history. Highlights include Bill and Betty Printy's blacksmith shop and gift store; the brick Federal-style Greef General Store; the Vernon School House (just across the Des Moines River), now an art gallery and home of artist-in-residence Wendell Mohr; and the Mason House Inn.

Built in 1846 by Mormon workmen who dropped out of the west-ward trek to Utah (temporarily, say the brochures, but we're not so easily convinced), the Mason House Inn is the oldest steamboat hotel in continuous use along the Des Moines River. Now owned

Modesty is a virtue, but cleanliness is next to godliness.

★ ★

and operated by Chuck and Joy Hanson as a bed-and-breakfast, the Mason House boasts a cookie jar in every room (each more or less full, depending on the willpower of the occupants) and is chock-full of antiques that were original to the hotel, including beds, dressers, an 1880 Buck's woodstove, an indoor well pump, and a Murphy tub.

Don't know what a Murphy tub is? Located in the Keeping Room at the back of the inn—the Keeping Room served as the family's living quarters—the Mason House Murphy tub is a fold-down, copper-lined tub that stows away in a cabinet in the wall when not in use. The only one of its kind in Iowa, the tub is in the middle of the room, right next to the fireplace so that water could be heated and added to the tub at will.

Depending on your level of comfort with your body and your inclinations toward exhibitionism, though, the Murphy tub is either a dream come true or your worst nightmare. There's no screen around the tub, and the chance of a little privacy in the Keeping Room, where the owners still do much of their living, is slim to none. If you do brave the waters, though, at least there'll be plenty of help around should you need someone to scrub your back.

The Mason House Inn is located at 21982 Hawk Drive, Bentonsport. For more information and reservations, call (319) 592-3133.

Come for the Artifacts, Marvel at the Display Cases
Bentonsport

When it comes to museums, it's rare for the wrapping to be as striking as the present. After all, you go to the Louvre to see the *Mona Lisa,* not to check out the drapes hanging in the windows. But in the case of Tony Sanders' Museum of Artifacts, Wood, and Horns, the log cabin and hand-built wooden display cases he painstakingly crafted to house his collection of over 4,000 arrowheads, mammoth teeth, and antlers are almost as impressive as their contents.

Sure, the axe heads and grinding stones and rows upon rows of arrowheads of every size and variety are wonderful. Tony collected

Wood paneling never looked so good. Tony Gray

them while "tramping around other people's property" in Van Buren and surrounding counties, and his museum, he says, is a way of giving back. But his wooden handiwork inside the building is truly stunning. For starters, he's covered every inch of the walls in a kind of repeating A-frame panel style that makes your run-of-the-mill wood paneling look downright lazy, featuring fourteen different kinds of locally harvested wood, from hickory to ash to mulberry to apple. Oh, and did we mention that he also paneled the floors, ceiling, and all the rafters in the same local-wood-super-sampler fashion? The display cases, too, feature unique designs made of hand-sawn inlaid wood, all of it varnished to a beautiful sheen. And with such stunning craftsmanship on display in the displays, you should be excused for forgetting to notice the arrowheads.

A self-described health nut who eats only wild game and fish, Tony grinds his own corn and wheat, jogs 5 miles a day, and bikes 20 miles back and forth to church on Sundays. His museum is usually open Saturdays and Sundays from mid-April to December if he's not out fishing or hunting (he's fond of squirrel), and Sundays the museum doesn't open until after Tony pedals the 10 miles back from church. Other times you might catch him by chance and he'll be happy to show you around, but don't expect him if we've just had a hard rain: According to Tony, that's the best time to walk the local creek beds, hunting arrowheads. Since he's already got plenty of them, we imagine he's just looking for an excuse to keep building those beautiful display cases.

Tony Sanders' Museum of Artifacts is located at 21929 Des Moines Street in Bentonsport. Admission is free but donations are accepted. Tony doesn't have a phone, but to check to see if he'll be around, you can call Bentonsport's Greef General Store at (319) 592-3579.

Twist and Turn on Snake Alley
Burlington

Even if your local road crews seem to have taken the last three years off and you've got many of your own hometown favorites in the bumpy and crooked road category, you'll still want to visit Burlington's Snake Alley, just about the crookedest and bumpiest street you're likely to ever find.

Reminiscent of San Francisco's Lombard Street and hailed by Ripley's Believe It or Not! as the crookedest street in the world, Snake Alley is composed of two quarter-turns and five half-turns carved into a steep hillside overlooking Burlington's downtown shopping district. Engineers and contractors built the street in 1894, laying each paving brick on its side and at a downward angle to provide horses better footing (and, hopefully, more horsepower) as they traversed the steep grade. (Legend has it that the Burlington Fire Department used Snake Alley to test the mettle of its horses.) The end result is a very steep street that looks like a coiled snake wearing a brick-ribbed sweater.

No longer open to street traffic except by permission, Snake Alley makes for a lovely winding walk 58 vertical feet down Heritage Hill to

★ ★

the shopping district below. Bordered by rough-cut granite walls and sculpted patches of fairway-green grass, the street is truly a beautiful piece of landscape architecture, winding its way beside a large red-brick church, the First United Church of Christ, and a number of well-preserved nineteenth-century homes.

All the tourist guidebooks celebrate this striking landmark of the Queen City, as Burlington used to be known, but the rest of the city is quite lovely, too, perched as it is on hills overlooking the Mississippi. Burlington is second only to Dubuque in terms of natural beauty—a view of the mighty river is never more than a few blocks away. But if you're anything like us, when it comes to sightseeing, nothing quite compares to some really good curves and bumps in the road.

Snake Alley runs between Washington and Columbia Streets on Sixth Street in downtown Burlington.

I Call the Top Outhouse!

Columbus City

The old three-room gas station George Bell bought and moved to the lot across the street from his house really draws sightseers, especially in the busy summer months: It's a quaint-looking white building with red trim, a nice front porch, and three towering red antique gas pumps out front. But it's the two-story outhouse in the side yard that really gets people out of their cars, not to mention scratching their heads.

So how did George come to find such a fine example of double-decker outhousedom? Well, truth be told, he didn't actually find it—he dreamt it up and built it himself. "I had an outhouse lying around and then someone gave me another one from Sigourney," he told me, "so I just cut the top off one and put the other on top of it."

The end result is a surprisingly realistic-looking two-story outhouse that makes perfect sense—one for the gents, one for the ladies—until you stop to think about it.

★ ★

I call top floor of the outhouse!

"Every once in a while I'll change the names above the doors," George said. "Sometimes the ladies are on the bottom, sometimes the gentlemen." And sometimes, he said, he'll put the names of politicians above the doors, depending on whoever happens to be out

★ ★

of favor and/or under investigation at the time. (There are always at least a couple of politicians in the proverbial outhouse, now aren't there?)

George's first love isn't outhouses, though, but old-fashioned gas stations, the kind that had a kitchen and a few stools out front so you could sit down while they made you a fried-egg sandwich. And he enjoys his visitors: "I have fun, they have fun," he told me. One word of advice if you do decide to stop by: Unless you're feeling especially adventurous, you may want to use the bathroom before you visit.

George Bell's place is located close to the corner of Philadelphia Street and Iowa Street in Columbus City.

Graffiti Barn Zen
Columbus Junction

Some people discover wisdom in the most unlikely of places. Bob Utter, for example, a farmer from Columbus Junction, found it on the broad side of a barn.

Utter rents farmland that sits about equidistant between three rival high schools: Columbus Junction, Wapello, and Muscatine. And one particular barn on his land happens to sit close to one of the most well-traveled highways in the area, with no farmhouse nearby to keep watch over it. And that, my friends, is how the graffiti barn was born.

"I had to really change my attitude," Bob explained. "I just had to change my mind." Years ago, when local high school kids first started painting the classic-looking wooden barn with sayings and slogans, Bob would get upset. He and his wife at first tried painting over the graffiti, but, unfortunately, they chose a nice graffiti-artist-tantalizing shade of white. After battling the kids for a while, Bob realized there was nothing he could do to stop them, and so instead of trying to change the kids, he changed his mind. "I just don't care anymore," he told me. "I just enjoy it."

★ ★

Who knew that high schoolers would be willing to paint the barn for free?

And there's a lot to enjoy. The barn is literally covered in a rainbow of graffiti that can change from week to week and sometimes, when high school rivalries are at a fever pitch, from night to night. "One day the barn will be covered in one school's colors, and the next day you wake up and it's painted entirely in another school's colors," Bob says.

Over the years he's developed a philosophy that sounds an awful lot like Graffiti Barn Zen. "I only make rules I can enforce now. My saying they couldn't paint the barn didn't do a thing. Now, if someone wants to paint the barn, they have my permission. One rule, though, is that the second you leave, anyone else who wants can paint right over it." Every once in a while he'll take a call from a disappointed artist whose work was covered up in a matter of days or even hours, and he'll have to remind him or her of his very sensible, and eminently enforceable, rule.

Another graffiti barn rule you might be surprised to learn is that people can paint anything they please, no matter how saintly or obscene. After all, how could Bob control what people choose to write? Such rules sound an awful lot like no rules, do they not, Grasshopper? This, my friend, is the mysterious and liberating power of Graffiti Barn Zen.

You'll find the graffiti barn a little over 6 miles east of Columbus Junction on the north side of IA 92. Since he can't really stop you, you have Bob's permission to paint his barn and, of course, you're free to write anything you want. But remember: This is Iowa, and even our graffiti artists tend to observe generally accepted standards of decorum.

A Swinging Good Bridge

Columbus Junction

It seems almost anywhere you go in this great big country, from Seattle, Washington, to Atlanta, Georgia, and everywhere in between, there's a legend about a lovesick Indian maiden leaping to her death off some local rock, cliff, or promontory. It's enough to make you wonder where all these suicidal Native American women came from. (And doesn't it make you wonder if modern psychopharmacology could have helped them be more resilient in the face of romantic setbacks?)

Columbus Junction's Swinging Bridge, a somewhat rickety-looking 262-foot suspension footbridge over a steep ravine between Third and Fourth Streets, is also known as Lovers Leap Bridge. Of course, the local lore has it that a heartbroken Indian woman may have used the bridge as a convenient spot to end her life after her lover died in battle. (The sign at the end of the bridge reads, "Did a lovesick Indian maiden leap to her death? The trees know and they won't tell." Those secretive trees . . .) The only trouble with the legend in

★ ★

this case is that the bridge really isn't that high up. But Lovers Two-Broken-Legs Leap doesn't have quite the same romantic ring to it, now does it?

Don't worry, this bridge hasn't collapsed in a long, long time.

No matter whether any lover has ever taken a leap off it, the bridge is still quite a sight and very fun to walk across since, true to its name, it swings back and forth with each step. Originally built in 1886, the Swinging Bridge has gone through a number of reconstructions and renovations, the most notable of which occurred after it collapsed while two people were walking across it in 1920. Don't worry, though: According to the same sign that mentions the maiden, neither person was hurt in the incident. But, come to think of it, that might be just another legend, too. Enjoy your walk across the bridge!

The Swinging Bridge is located between Third and Fourth Streets in Columbus Junction. Look for the sign on IA 92 just west of downtown.

Why Would You Set Your Sister Up with Your Dentist?
Eldon

Before we share this curiosity, you have to promise one thing: If you go, have your picture taken wearing the funny clothes out front. We know, we know, you'll feel silly; the clothes (or half clothes really, since they only shoot you from the waist up) might be a little too big or too small, and who wants to look like such a hopeless tourist? Please, just have your picture taken. After all, how often do you get to parody the most recognizable Iowans in history? And the pictures are just as sweet as apple pie.

We're talking about the photo they'll take of you, if you're willing, in front of the American Gothic House in Eldon. Grant Wood used the house as the model for the backdrop to his painting *American Gothic*, which he entered into an Art Institute of Chicago competition in 1930 (he won $300) and which is still one of the most famous and recognizable paintings in American art.

You know the painting: In the background is a white farmhouse, its most notable feature a gothic window with arched mullions. (Wood, when he first saw the window on a scouting mission for things to paint, thought it rather pretentious for such a plain-looking house.) And in the foreground is a balding and bespectacled man dressed in what looks to be a suit jacket and overalls, his right hand grasping a pitchfork. Beside him stands a woman much younger than he, her blond hair pulled back, dressed in a brown frock with a broach fastened at her neck. But their faces are the gravitational center of the painting, the thing that pulls us in and holds our gaze. Who are they? What's their relationship to one another? Are they stern? Proud? Tired? Wary?

Grant's models for the pair were his sister and his dentist. Take your pick, but dress up as one of them and have your picture taken. Do your best to imitate those inscrutable and intense gazes, and then check the visitor center's Web site to see if your parody made the grade.

The American Gothic House, and the newly constructed visitor center, are located at 300 American Gothic Street in Eldon. For more information, call (641) 652-3352 or visit www.wapellocounty.org/americangothic. And be sure to check out those pictures.

So This Is How You Attain Perfect Knowledge
Fairfield

When it comes to the challenge of finding curiosities in Iowa, the little town of Fairfield is like a really slow pitch sent smack-dab down the middle of the plate. This town of 10,000, which boasts a classic Norman Rockwell–style town square, is so off-the-charts unusual, it's probably easier to describe the handful of ways in which it's ordinary (it is, after all, surrounded by lots and lots of corn) than to list the many ways it will defy your every expectation about small-town Iowa.

Just for starters, instead of being home to, say, a dirt-track motor speedway, Fairfield boasts one of the world's premier Ayurvedic health spas, the Raj. (Ayurvedic means the Raj's treatment regimens are based on the ancient Hindu science of health and medicine.) After your royal treatment, head downtown for a bite, where you'll

Who knew knowledge of the universe could be had so easily?

find more restaurants per capita than San Francisco, with no less than three Indian restaurants and a grand total of nine restaurants or cafes that bill themselves as "vegan friendly." After your meal, be sure to check out one of the twenty-plus art galleries on the town square.

And did we mention there's a university in town called the Maharishi University of Management, which offers degrees in ordinary things like elementary education and mathematics, but where students and faculty also practice compulsory Transcendental Meditation and "yogic flying," a meditation technique that involves sitting on a foam mat with one's legs in a pretzel-like lotus position and then periodically "frog-hopping" up and down a little bit? Like we said: Nice and slow, right over the plate.

★ ★

Most of Fairfield's wonderful uniqueness can be attributed to one man, Maharishi Mahesh Yogi, who brought his trademarked technique of Transcendental Meditation to the West in the late 1950s and gained his greatest fame in the 1960s as spiritual guru to the Beatles. (*Maharishi* means "Great Seer" in Hindi, a name Mahesh Prasad Varma bestowed upon himself.) The organization he founded in order to spread the ancient Hindu principles of perfect health and world peace made its home in Fairfield, with the Maharishi University of Management its centerpiece. All the galleries and restaurants and yogic flying followed.

In 2001 disciples of Maharishi's movement created Iowa's newest town just 2 miles north of Fairfield, Maharishi Vedic City, where all homes are built according to Ayurvedic architectural principles, a kind of Indian version of feng shui. Among a whole slew of specialized architectural details intended to promote health, well-being, and peace, every building in the town faces east and features a central silent space called a *brahmasthan* and a golden roof ornament called a *kalash*. The city also boasts a one-and-a-half-acre open-air observatory called the Maharishi Vedic Observatory, featuring ten large masonry astronomical instruments that look like modern art and which will, according to the Vedic City Web site, help the visitor understand the structure and laws of the universe. If you're not tempted to visit Fairfield and Maharishi Vedic City for the wonderful art or organic food or yogic flying, wouldn't you just love to be the first in your neighborhood to understand the structure of the universe?

Maharishi Vedic City, a town so healthful that it banned the sale of nonorganic food, is located 2 miles north of Fairfield just off IA 1. Call the Raj for visitor information at (641) 472-9580 or visit www .maharishivediccity-iowa.gov.

Cones and Kids on the Outside

Fort Madison

If a 20-foot-tall concrete soft-serve ice-cream cone and a concrete giraffe don't make a strange enough sight for you, try tossing into the mix a 50-foot-tall guard tower and you'll begin to get a sense of what a surreal place the ice-cream stand at the northwestern corner of Fort Madison State Penitentiary truly is. The gothic guard tower and the almost laughably huge, depressing, and dispiriting prison walls (made of drab gray stone, more than 35 feet tall in places, supported by giant buttresses) are mere yards away from this soft-serve ice-cream stand, 18-hole miniature golf course, and batting cage. (Batters face the prison walls—do they imagine they are knocking a home run right into the "pen"?)

An ice-cream stand with a strong anticrime message. Catherine Cole

★ ★

Step right up (under surveillance, of course) and order a cone from an apple-cheeked youngster. Lick your cone, watch the kids frolic on the Astroturf, and try not to be distracted by the coils of concertina wire over your left shoulder or the shadows at your feet cast by the looming prison walls. And not just any prison walls. Fort Madison State Penitentiary, a maximum-security prison, was originally built in 1839, before Iowa even attained statehood. There've been many additions and renovations since then, of course, but the original cellblock is still in use, and three of the prison houses are on the National Register of Historic Places. (As a side note, we suggest you avoid historic prisons should you ever decide to get incarcerated. Historic homes, good; historic prisons, bad.)

The penitentiary's overall effect makes Alcatraz look like Fantasy Island, but it's probably the only maximum-security prison in the country, and perhaps in the world, where you can bring the kids to the prison walls and make a night of it, putting for par, swinging for the bleachers (or the guardhouse), and finishing it all off with an ice-cream sundae, two cherries on top. Could Midwestern leisure get any weirder?

Fort Madison State Penitentiary and the ice-cream stand are on US 61, just northwest of downtown Fort Madison.

A Cursed Statue with a Prudish Streak
Iowa City

If it weren't for all those graves, you might confuse Iowa City's Oakland Cemetery for a well-designed park. The land rises and falls to form gentle knolls and valleys; mature maple, oak, and cedar trees line the narrow asphalt roads; and the lawns are brilliantly green and impeccably groomed three seasons of the year. The cemetery's eastern edge abuts Hickory Hill Park, and dog walkers and joggers are a common sight among the headstones as they make their way to sniff and/or pound the park's trails.

Doesn't sound very spooky, does it? But wait: We forgot to mention that in the middle of the cemetery is an infamous cursed statue,

An angel with a heavy heart—and a possible case of osteoporosis.

a towering, 9-foot-tall black angel, her massive bronze wings folded earthward, her heavy head hanging low, looking so downtrodden and weary you'll want to help her off her cold pedestal and put her to rest.

Don't offer her your sympathy so fast, though. Among the many legends surrounding the so-called Black Angel is that any girl kissed near her in the moonlight will die within six months. Another myth has it that anyone who kisses the statue dies instantly. Yet another

says that the Black Angel turned black (it's original color was bronze) and continues to have such ill effects on people because of a wife's infidelity. Come to think of it, almost every legend surrounding her has something to do with kissing and death, in that order. Whoever or whatever the Black Angel is, one thing is sure: She's reputed to be a strong, and strong-handed, advocate of abstinence, at least in her cemetery.

One true story concerning the Black Angel is that she was commissioned by a Czech midwife, Teresa Dolezal Feldevert, who emigrated to Iowa City in the late nineteenth century, to mark the graves of her second husband, Nicholas Feldevert, and her son, Eddie Dolezal, who died at age eighteen. When Teresa died in 1924, she too was buried in the shadow of the Black Angel's massive wings. One of the many peculiarities of the tomb, however, is that although Mrs. Feldevert's year of birth is engraved on the base, her year of death is absent, as if she were still alive. Even more unusual is the Black Angel's position: Whereas most angels on tombstones are depicted with heads and wings uplifted to symbolize the soul's ascent into heaven, the Black Angel, shoulders slumped, wings folded downward, looks like Atlas carrying the weight of the world on her back.

Perhaps the least mysterious aspect of the legend surrounding the Black Angel is why she turned black. (Curious citizens have chipped away at some of the black in places, trying to catch a glimpse of what's underneath.) The answer: good old-fashioned oxidation of the bronze in which she was cast. But your guess is as good as ours as to why the Black Angel is so dead-set against a little kissing.

At the corner of Brown and Governor Streets, Oakland Cemetery is open from 7:00 a.m. to 9:00 p.m. seven days a week. After you enter the main gate, follow the asphalt path east until you see the Black Angel.

★ ★

Long Journey with No Baggage Check
Iowa City

Just prior to the Civil War, Iowa City was the soon-to-be-completed transcontinental railroad's western terminus. If you traveled any farther west, across the prairie and onward to the Great Plains, to seek land, fortune, and/or adventure, you couldn't do it in cushioned comfort at an even 40 or 50 miles per hour. Instead, you went by horse and wagon (preferably covered), and the ride was bumpier, longer, hotter, and more perilous than we can probably imagine.

Or, if you were Mormon, you proved your mettle by avoiding conveyances entirely and traveling by foot, pulling all your worldly possessions behind you in a homemade handcart. In May 1856 the first of a group of 1,900 British and Scandinavian members of the Church of Jesus Christ of Latter-Day Saints, or Mormons, arrived in Iowa City and set up camp on the western edge of town. Their ultimate goal was Salt Lake City, Utah, more than 1,300 miles away, but they had a few minor challenges to overcome before they got there, not the least of which was that they were too poor to buy horses, wagons, or even handcarts.

When the Mormon leader, Brigham Young, heard of their plight, he was reported to have said, "Let them come on foot, with handcarts or wheelbarrows, let them gird up their loins and walk through." And that's exactly what they did, making their own handcarts, loading up their possessions (each person was allowed seventeen pounds of belongings), and walking from Iowa City to Utah in five separate handcart companies that averaged about 15 miles a day throughout the spring, summer, and early fall.

Mormon Handcart Park, an unassuming gem of a park tucked behind university athletic fields off Mormon Trek Boulevard, marks the spot of the original encampment, which, the placards tell us, looks much the same as it did when the Mormons were preparing for their journey. The park is located at the end of Hawkeye Court Road, off Mormon Trek Boulevard. For more information, call (319) 335-1050.

★ ★

Old-Fashioned Taxidermy
Iowa City

Where can you go to find a 13-foot giant sloth wearing a Santa suit, a 46-foot right-whale skeleton, and a hummingbird egg about as big as your thumbnail? If you're in Iowa City, the answer is MacBride Hall, located a few steps northeast of the Old Capitol on the university's Pentacrest and home to the University of Iowa's Museum of Natural History. The museum's oldest galleries, Mammal Hall and the William and Eleanor Hageboeck Hall of Birds, both located on the third floor, have been in existence since 1858, making the Museum of Natural History the oldest university museum west of the Mississippi.

But if mere old age isn't enough to tempt you, then consider this: Over a century ago a museum of natural history meant one thing:

A sloth who knows how to party.

lots and lots of exotic dead animals. Mammal Hall contains hundreds of them, including a panther, a zebra, a rhino (complete with dried mud on his back), a wolf, a wombat, and an aardvark, down the great chain of being to lowly squirrels and mice (at least a dozen different varieties of each), all killed and then stuffed for the sole purpose of being displayed in dioramas of the Serengeti or the Arctic or the less exotic Iowa countryside. Don't miss standing directly under the massive ribs of the right whale suspended from the hall's ceiling; the skeleton alone weighs in at 4,000 pounds.

More than a thousand stuffed birds fill Bird Hall, including a remarkable glass case of over one hundred different bird eggs, a peacock in mesmerizing tail spread, and a nearly 360-degree diorama, or cyclorama, of a South Pacific island, complete with a gaggle or two of stuffed native birds in the foreground.

There have been a few attempts to make the museum a little more twenty-first century, including a large diorama of the dramatic ecological changes humans have wrought in Iowa, the state where, the caption says, "people have altered the landscape more dramatically than any other." But for the most part, the third-floor halls have remained pure nineteenth century, and it's enough to make a visitor reel from science culture shock.

The museum's main exhibit space is on MacBride's first floor, Iowa Hall, a gallery that explores 500 million years of Iowa's ecology, geology, and cultural history. Here you'll find what museum coordinator David Brenzel lovingly refers to as "our star," a towering giant sloth, bizarre snout in the air, massive claws reaching for the foliage on some tree from the Ice Age. (If you come at the right time, you might find him dressed for the season as a pilgrim or even jolly old St. Nick.)

MacBride Hall is located downtown on the University of Iowa's Pentacrest, at the corner of Iowa Avenue and Clinton Street. For more information, including hours of operation, call (319) 335-0480 or visit www.uiowa.edu/~nathist/index.html.

★ ★

A Shopper's Orgy
Iowa City

If you're looking to buy a hundred-year-old deer rifle, a silver mercury dime from the 1930s, and a loaf of bread from a Mennonite farmer named Cephis Yoder, there's only one place for you to go: Iowa City's Sharpless Auction. Held every Wednesday night from 5:30 p.m. to around 9:00 p.m., it's the state's biggest indoor auction, averaging 400 bidders in winter and more than twice that in the peak summer months, when the better merchandise arrives.

And, oh, the merchandise! Fresh-from-the-old-farmhouse goods run the gamut from green vinyl couches to covet-fit-inducing antique oak dressers, from headless Barbie dolls to grandma's heirloom china. Everything you'd ever dream of finding in an old attic, garage, bedroom, kitchen, or barn is here, spread out on tables and along the walls in no particular order, at least none that we could decipher.

Grab your auction number, stand by your find, and size up the competition as you wait for the auctioneer on the podium to move the bidding from the front to the back of the room. Remember, only novices raise a number early, since the auctioneer tends to start the bid laughably high. (Why does he talk so fast, and why does that high-speed, tongue-twirling drone make us so eager to buy?) And be sure to keep your Midwestern hospitality in check: One errant wave to a neighbor at the Mennonite baked-goods table might mean you'll go home with a musty feather boa you'll never, ever wear.

Sharpless Auctions is on I-80, just off exit 249, the first exit east of Iowa City. Auctions take place on Wednesday nights and begin at 5:30 p.m.

An Autobiography in Clocks
Lockridge

To call Johnny McLain's hand-carved wooden creations "clocks" doesn't quite do them justice. They're more like fine-art installations

These clocks do a whole lot more than tell time.

with a clock tucked in as an afterthought among all the elaborate carvings and myriad objects from his past. Telling time isn't so much the goal here as telling a story in wood and glass—Johnny's story. And what a beautifully crafted and "timely" tale it is.

His "clock" titled *Memories,* to offer just one example, contains an antique treasure trove of things from Johnny's childhood. There's an old banjo and violin, a lamp that once belonged to Johnny's mother, an old-fashioned telephone and mantel clock from his boyhood home, old ribbons, a toy train car, numerous small hand tools, and quite a few buttons collected from the Midwest Old Threshers Show. All this and more is displayed in a glass-front wooden "clock" the size of a convenience store beverage cooler, accented by porch posts and a thick crown of hand-carved wooden leaves. (To say there's a lot going on here is an understatement: If you happened to be

★ ★

looking at the clock when someone casually asked you the time, you could be forgiven for taking a long time to answer.) Even the wood the piece is made from has special significance for Johnny: "That clock is made from some of the last wood my brother sawed before he died and the last wood my father sawed before he died."

Not all of the pieces in the Johnny Clock Museum, located in a large room off the backside of the home Johnny shares with wife Pat, are quite as personal (and as full of memorabilia) as *Memories*. But each one of the more than fifty stunning hand-carved clocks provides a window into Johnny's life and passions. There's a Walt Disney clock, filled with tiny wooden carvings of Disney characters; a Grand Ol' Opry clock, shaped like an antique wooden radio with the clock face tucked into the body of a violin; and an Old Country Home clock, containing a carved miniature model of the farmstead where Johnny grew up.

"Growing up, I had what they now call dyslexia," Johnny told me, "so I couldn't really learn to read and write." In his early twenties, after traveling the country by boxcar and doing odd jobs along the way, he began to worry he'd never be able to support himself. That's about the time he came back to Lockridge and rediscovered his skill for carving. He eventually earned a living as a master restorer of antique furniture, work he and Pat still do today. And since his wonderful talent lies in wood and not in words, he chose to write the story of his life in clocks. "I lived it," he said, "and then I carved what I lived." And then he put a clock somewhere inside it.

Johnny says he gets no greater joy than when a child who's having trouble in school visits his museum. "I tell them God gives every one of us some talent, some way to provide for ourselves, and it's up to us to find what it is." Don't be afraid of making mistakes, he tells them, and then he laughs and points out a few of his own—he works without written plans and has ended up carving a few numbers and letters on the clocks backwards. A mistake so well executed, though, doesn't really look like a mistake. And maybe, come to think of it, that's exactly Johnny's point.

The Johnny Clock Museum is located about a mile west of downtown Lockridge on West Main Street. Call Pat and Johnny at (319) 696-3711 to set up an appointment.

Buttons of Yesteryear
Muscatine

Around the turn of the last century, Muscatine produced more than 1.5 billion buttons per year, nearly 40 percent of the world's annual supply. At the height of production, more than forty factories stamped button blanks out of mussel shells dragged from the Mississippi River, which were then finished in home workshops scattered throughout the city. Townspeople produced so many buttons that in a moment of uncharacteristic Iowa boastfulness, Muscatine dubbed itself the "Pearl Button Capital of the World."

The Pearl Button Museum is a downtown Muscatine storefront devoted to the history of what was once the area's biggest industry. You'll learn about the inventive and enterprising German immigrant John Boepple, who discovered that mussels from the Mississippi worked just as well as the more costly animal horns traditionally used for button making. Thanks to his ingenuity, between 1885 and 1910 Mississippi River mussels were bivalvular gold for communities all the way from Marquette south to Keokuk, providing Boepple and others with the raw material needed to keep half the world's shirts and dresses fastened for another year. The museum features beautiful old photographs, loads of buttons, and probably more details than you might care to know about the process of making buttons out of shells at the turn of the century.

Plastic spelled the end of Muscatine's button-making braggadocio, and a bustling industry vanished almost overnight. If you don't believe a whole museum could be dedicated to such a mundane but serviceable object as the button and still be more interesting than yard work, the Pearl Button Museum will prove you wrong.

The Pearl Button Museum is located in the heart of downtown, at

Radio Demagogue and Quack Norman Baker

Most towns memorialize their most admirable and honorable citizens: war heroes, suffragists, civic leaders. Muscatine, though, boldly bucked this trend and decided instead to immortalize a homegrown charlatan on a small plaque on top of a hill at the corner of Second and Brook.

While the front of the plaque features a quote from Mark Twain (who used to spend summers in Iowa) about how beautiful the sunsets are in Muscatine, the back notes that the site was the location of Muscatine's first radio station, KTNT, or Know the Naked Truth, founded by Norman Baker himself.

In many ways it was a typical AM station of the 1920s, with programming that featured chamber concerts, inspirational readings, and Baker's daily rants. But by running huge copper cables from his homemade transmitter all the way down the hill to the Mississippi, Baker turned the Big Muddy into a giant reflector for his radio signal, located at 1170 on the AM dial. In doing so he paid nominal heed to FCC-imposed broadcasting power limits; some old-timers claim that on winter nights, KTNT could be heard halfway across the country.

Baker also spent a fair amount of airtime advertising a miracle cure for cancer, available only at the "hospital" he himself headed. Since effective treatments for cancer were virtually nonexistent in those days, dying patients were willing to try anything, including a stay at Baker's hospital, where morning lines for admission sometimes stretched around the block. How successful were the treatments? Some say the number of bodies taken away by hearse after dark each night roughly equaled the number of daily admits. The radio station kept new customers coming from near and far, and to this day no one knows how much money Baker made off the enterprise.

It wasn't long before both the American Medical Association and the FCC began pressuring Baker to close up shop. Finally, in 1931 the FCC pulled his license, putting an end to both KTNT and Baker's "medical career" in Iowa. Undeterred, Baker repaired to Hot Springs, Arkansas; bought an old hotel; and went back into the radio and cancer-treatment businesses. Later, when he was asked to leave Arkansas, he moved just across the Mexican border and set up a 100,000-watt station that, if conditions were right, could be heard clearly back in Muscatine.

By the time Norman Baker died, he was so reviled in his hometown that when his body arrived for burial in the family plot, the funeral director had to go to the local community college and pay six students $5 apiece to serve as pallbearers. And if the plaque mentioning Baker and his infamous radio station at the Mark Twain Overlook is the result of a little old-fashioned palm greasing, too, no one's talking.

The plaque is located at the Mark Twain Overlook on the hill just south of downtown Muscatine at Second and Brook Streets. For additional information, call (563) 263-0241.

117 West Second Street. Admission is free, but donations are gladly accepted. The museum is open Tuesday through Saturday from 10:00 a.m. to 4:00 p.m. or by appointment. Call (563) 263-1052 or visit www.pearlbutton.org for more information.

Caught between the Moon and Iowa
Muscatine

Want an exotic vacation but don't quite have the cash to get to Cairo? A close or distant second, depending on your affinity for kitsch, might be a stay at the Econo Lodge Fantasuite Motel, located on the northern edge of Muscatine, a delightful Mississippi River town about 27 miles south of the Quad Cities. It's lowbrow luxury, of course, but we Iowans tend to be a practical people. After all, why spend a mattress full of money on pricey hotels, fancy food, and tours when you can stick close to home and just pretend you've gone somewhere instead?

Indulge yourself in any one of a number of fantasies, depending on your mood. Feeling a little intergalactic? Then slip into the moon-crater whirlpool in the Space Odyssey Suite. Or, if it suits your fantasy, raise the dead in the Pharaoh's Chamber. For the weary traveler the Arabian Nights Suite offers desert-oasis accommodations, not to mention an octagonal bed. All suites feature whirlpool baths and romantic extras, in a mirrors-on-the-ceiling sort of way.

That charge you hear leveled against so many hotel rooms—that they all look the same, whether you're in Des Moines or Saigon—certainly doesn't apply here. If you're the type who feels most comfortable with the mundane, though, the motel also offers everyday rooms at a more modest price. (It's never cheap to indulge your fantasies, even close to home.) If you play it safe, be sure to take the suite tours offered Sundays at 3:00 p.m. so that you can at least get a glance at the spaceship bed and see how the Jetson-set lives.

The hotel is located at 2402 Park Avenue on the northern edge of town. For more information or reservations, call (563) 264-3337.

★ ★

Mecca for Trekkies

Riverside

Ever wonder why the USS *Enterprise,* the spaceship from the TV show *Star Trek,* undertook such a long and dangerous journey? Why all the expense and trouble and the five long years, why the countless teleporter and warp-drive headaches for Scotty down in engineering, why all of Captain Kirk's torn polyester shirts, and, most important, why all the fraternizing with hordes of heavily makeupped, scantily clad alien women? Was it really just "to explore strange new worlds, to seek out new life forms and new civilizations, to boldly go where no man has gone before"?

Of course not. It was to help Captain Kirk get the heck out of Iowa. According to Gene Rodenberry's book, *The Making of Star*

Though it might look like a famous starship, licensing fees can be outrageous. It's really the USS *Riverside*.

★ ★

Trek, Captain James T. Kirk "was born in a small town in the state of Iowa" in the year 2228, and by the year 2250 Kirk was a Starfleet graduate on his first assignment, out of town, out of state, out of the galaxy, and getting farther away from home every nanosecond.

Riverside, just east of Kalona, is the small Iowa town that claims the official but dubious privilege of being the future birthplace of the smirking, leg-crossing fictional hero all too anxious to put as many light years as possible between himself and his old eastern Iowa stomping grounds. After contacting Rodenberry about the idea in 1985 at the prompting of a local Trek fan, the town council received a certificate from the show's creator confirming Riverside's birthplace status by dint of the fact that they were the first town to ask. Now, every summer on the last Saturday in June, Riverside celebrates Trek Fest, and thousands of *Star Trek* fanatics, or Trekkies, travel to town to dress up as Klingons and Starfleet officers, watch videos of the show, hold fan-club meetings, buy and sell show memorabilia, drink beer, and have a parade down Main Street.

The town hoped to construct a bronze bust of Kirk to give due homage to their future wanderer, but Paramount wanted a $40,000 licensing fee to use Kirk's future likeness, and that was that. Instead, they built their very own starship, the USS *Riverside* (a station-wagon-size *Enterprise* knockoff), and set it down on a trailer in a small park downtown, as if the teleporter weren't working and the crew had been forced to make a rare trailer landing.

Young people have been leaving small towns in Iowa in search of greener pastures for decades. Many head for Minneapolis or Chicago, some go much farther, and a sizable number even eventually return home to enjoy the very same things that, as teenagers, they couldn't wait to leave behind. But Riverside has the honor of inspiring a fictional future son to flee farther and faster from Iowa than any man has fled before. The best we can hope for is that he at least remembers to call his poor mom back in Riverside to wish her happy birthday.

Riverside is located 13 miles south of Iowa City on IA 22. You can't miss the 22-foot-long USS *Riverside* in the small park downtown. Trek Fest is held each year on the last Saturday in June. For more information, call (319) 648-5475 or visit www.trekfest.com.

Pardon Me, Could You Please Pass the Minnows?
Wapello

These days the restaurant business is tougher than tough: profit margins are low, food prices are high and rising, and belt-tightening customers are eating at home more (and, hence, eating out less) to try to save a few precious bucks. Depending on your perspective, and on your comfort with the idea of live bait just a tiny tail flip away from your biscuits and gravy, Bill and Dianna Petty, owners of the Honey Hole Diner in Wapello, have either discovered a brilliant antidote to the restaurateur blues or made things a whole lot harder on themselves.

Don't worry, the minnows can't see you eating your catfish.

★ ★

"Sure, I've had people come into the diner to eat and then walk right back out," Bill tells me when I ask him about the challenges of running a bait and tackle shop and sit-down diner in the very same room. "Some people just won't eat with minnows." As if we needed another reminder that narrow-mindedness takes oh-so-many forms.

It's been two years since Bill and Dianna bought the Honey Hole from the previous owner, and in that time Bill's faced head-on (or should we say nose-on?) the primary drawback of having four large tanks of minnows in the middle of his restaurant: the whiff of something fishy going on. "When I first took over, there wasn't hardly a woman in town would come into this place," he said. "And it was because of the smell." He now cleans the tanks twice a week to prevent odor, even though the minnows only need their tanks cleaned about once a month—they're a lot less picky, apparently, than the women of Wapello.

He also keeps the little guys covered with camouflage tarps, so you don't have to see them looking at you forlornly during Friday's catfish-fry lunch. And fair warning: Be sure to get there early for the catfish because there's almost always a line. If they run out, though, don't worry. All the food on the menu is from-scratch homemade and absolutely delicious (most of it courtesy of Dianna Petty), from the huge biscuits to the towering lemon meringue pie to the gigantic pancakes. "There's very few people who can finish two of our pancakes," Bill says. We'll take that as a challenge.

"The place is geared more towards the sportsman, of course," Bill said. "But I've got more little old ladies that come in during the week than you would ever think." The bait and tackle shop does a brisk business year-round, too, but it's especially busy in summer. And not a single one of Bill's customers who comes in to buy, say, two dozen of his minnows (he pond traps them himself) or a bag of his own hand-poured weights has ever complained about the admittedly powerful smell of coffee, eggs, and bacon.

The Honey Hole Diner with Bait & Tackle Shop is located at 507

Highway 61 North in Wapello. The tackle shop is open Monday through Friday from 5:30 a.m. to 5:30 p.m., Saturday 5:30 a.m. to 4:00 p.m., and Sunday 5:30 a.m. to noon. Diner hours are Monday through Saturday from 6:00 a.m. to 2:00 p.m. and Sunday 6:00 a.m. to 11:00 a.m. For more information, call (319) 523-3834.

Is It Just Me, or Is This Ham a Little Tough?
Wapello

Less than a block away from the Honey Hole Diner is another culinary marvel that you shouldn't miss, this one encased in glass and totally unfit for consumption, unless you have a really close friend who's a dentist. A once-famous petrified ham, perhaps the only one in existence, rests regally on a Christmas-red piece of felt in a below-knee-level lighted display case in the Louisa County Historical Museum.

The museum contains lots of historical stuff besides the petrified ham, of course, including Native American dioramas from the Toolsboro Indian Mounds site, sprouting tiny model-train-set trees; a beautiful old kitchen stove; and a whole secondhand-store's worth of antique clothing, mostly from the period between the two World Wars. But the museum's crowning jewel, at least in this observer's eye, is George Kern's petrified ham.

Now let's be up front: Naysayers have it that the ham is nothing more than a chunk of brown rock that just happens to be in the shape of a ham. But if you believe even half the stories told about the petrified piece of pork (or pork impostor), you'll have to admit it's had an illustrious life worthy of a fossilized piece of meat ten times its size.

Legend has it that pioneers dropped the ham as they crossed the Iowa River near the town of Oakville, and over the many decades it sat on the riverbed, it slowly turned to stone. Then one George Kern got hold of it, and that's when the fun really started.

Kern owned a grocery store in nearby Columbus City in the 1930s, and he proudly displayed his fossilized ham on a wooden counter,

★ ★

A very well-preserved piece of pork.

pointing out its many ham-like details, from the white streaks of fat to what he claimed was a little hunk of bone. "During the past several months or since I have become owner of the 'Ham,'" George Kern wrote in 1937, "over 10,000 people from 40 states . . . have called at our home in Columbus City, Iowa, to see and examine the 'Ham,' and most all of these people have pronounced it to be the most wonderful specimen in the line of petrified objects that they ever seen." Kern even had visitors sign a ham registry and guess the weight, a whopping fifty-seven pounds—and reportedly only 27 people out of 10,000-plus got it right. According to Columbus City's George Bell, the ham was so popular that Kern's stack of registers filled with the names of petrified ham groupies stood an impressive 3 feet high.

★ ★

Mr. Kern died in the 1950s, and in the intervening years the ham passed from one Kern relative to another until it finally ended up at the Louisa County Museum—an old Iowa celebrity trying to make a comeback. Sadly, these days there seems to be a lot less interest in petrified meat among our young people. But, honestly, don't we all still love a solid piece of ham?

You'll find the Louisa County Historical Society Museum, and George Kern's petrified ham, at 509 Highway 61 North. Call (319) 527-5247 for hours and additional information.

The Finest Round Barn Around
West Branch

Ever wonder what mid-nineteenth-century farmers argued about? Barns, for starters. More specifically, they debated the costs and benefits of round barns versus the tried and true rectangular variety. As part of a larger effort to promote more efficient and economical farming practices, Iowa State University encouraged area farmers and contractors to build round barns, but Iowans weren't so easily convinced. Was it mere folly to build in the round, or did a true round, or eight-, or sixteen-sided barn stand up to tornadoes better, as well as offer more storage space bang for the materials buck? (And that debate, my friends, might be indicative of the excitement of life on a nineteenth-century Iowa farm.)

Just take a glance at almost any barn still around, and you'll know which side (or how many sides) won. In Iowa the squares have it by a long shot. Between 1830 and 1920 farmers built an estimated 100,000 barns in the state, but only 180 were round or multisided. At present, barns are reported to be disappearing from the Iowa landscape at the rate of about 1,000 per year, and only about a hundred of the round and multisided barns remain.

The Secrest Octagonal Barn, located just west of Downey, is said to be one of Iowa's largest and finest remaining round barns. (Of course, it's not really round but eight-sided. In Iowa, though, more

than four sides earn a barn honorary round status.) Built in 1883 by a master builder with the unlikely name of George Longerbeam (we didn't make that up), the barn is 80 feet tall and once held more than 200 tons of hay in the loft, along with thirty-two horses, sixteen cows, and farm implements galore in the lower level. It also features classic red vertical siding, a sectional bell-shaped roof, and an octagonal cupola that sits six stories above the barnyard.

Thanks to the efforts of a local professor, Richard Tyler, and scores of volunteers, the barn is in sound round shape for its age. Just pull up and take a gander. There are no regular tours because it's not a business but a private passion shared by Tyler and a select group of interested citizens. If you show up, you've automatically joined the latter group. Don't be shy; the owner is used to having company. But be forewarned: If you stay around much longer than half an hour, he'll probably slap a bucket in your hand and put you to work.

The Secrest Octagonal Barn is located at 5750 Osage Street in West Liberty, about 10 miles east of Iowa City and 5 miles south of West Branch. From Iowa City head east on US 6 about 5 miles. At the bend in the road turn left on Oasis Road, go 1 mile, and turn right on Osage Street. The barn will be about 1 mile down the road on left.

Hoover's Morning Medicine
West Branch

There are most certainly some benefits to being the president of the United States. When West Branch's most famous son, Herbert Hoover, began his term in 1928, he was a little chunky, about 210 pounds on a 5-foot, 11-inch frame. But instead of scolding him, or telling him to cut carbs (did they know about carbs back then?), his physician, Joel T. Boone, invented a game to help Hoover stay trim and even invited his cabinet to play it with him, first thing every morning (except Sundays, of course).

And what a game it was. Christened "Hoover Ball" by a *New York Times* reporter, it consisted of teams of two to four, an 8-foot-high net, a 66-by-30-foot court, and a six-pound medicine ball. The rules were simple: Catch the ball on your side of the net (trying not to grunt) and throw it immediately back over at your opponents, preferably as hard and fast as humanly possible. The *Des Moines Register* caught the spirit of the game when it reported: "The effect is that of a group of travelers tossing their luggage at a boat that has just pulled away from the dock, only to have the crew heave it right back again." Scored just like tennis but decidedly less genteel, Hoover Ball became something of a sensation during Hoover's term—people were throwing medicine balls at one another all across the country.

Hoover and his so-called Medicine Ball Cabinet were fanatical about the game. Each morning, rain or shine, a group of four to eighteen dignitaries (with an average age of fifty-three) showed up on the White House lawn dressed in flannel shirts, leather jackets, and old trousers and played Hoover Ball until the 7:30 a.m. whistle blew at a factory nearby. "We paid no attention to the weather except for a very heavy rain," wrote Secretary of the Interior Ray Lyman Wilbur. "We played in cold and wind, snow and rain, and in the four years we were driven indoors only two or three times [to play in the White House basement!] because of an unusually drenching downpour." Reports had it that Hoover was a "lusty" Hoover Ball player, with a mean forehand drive, but that Supreme Court justice and former Columbia football star Harlan F. Stone was a positive menace. "When he hurls them," one observer claimed, "they stay hurled."

But enough of history. Hoover Ball is still alive and well, right here in West Branch. Every August during Hooverfest, a celebration in honor of President Hoover's birthday, the Hoover Ball National Championships are held. Anyone—that's right, even you—can field a team and compete for a national title in either the four-pound or six-pound medicine-ball categories. Or, of course, if getting hit in the gut over and over again with a medicine ball isn't your idea of a good time, you can just go and cheer on your favorite lusty Hoover Baller.

★ ★

And how good was Hoover Ball at keeping Hoover trim? He dropped to a svelte 185 during his term and never missed a day of work due to illness or medicine-ball-related injury. Still, some people aren't sold on the game. *Sports Illustrated* complained that heaving a six-pound ball back and forth over an 8-foot-high net "cannot be accomplished graciously." Though that may be true, we know people will do far less gracious things to drop a few pounds. For example, have you ever had to watch someone eat a hamburger without a bun?

The Hoover Presidential Library in West Branch hosts Hooverfest the first week of August in honor of Hoover's birthday. The Hoover Ball National Championships are held in West Branch's Beranek Park. For more information or for entry forms, call (800) 828-0475 or visit www.hooverassociation.org/hooverball.html.

What'll It Be? A Dipsy Doodle or a Hadacol?

Wilton

Established in 1867 and billed as the nation's oldest continuously operating soda fountain, the Wilton Candy Kitchen offers visitors an almost surreal dose of authentic Americana, which is a fancy way of saying that the place is so real it's unreal. Little has changed in the shop since the 1920s, when the current owner, George Nopoulos, started working for his father at the age of six, winding the Bruns-wick record player to keep customers entertained. The high stamped-tin ceiling, white marble countertops (burnished by more than a hundred years of elbow rubbing), walnut booths, leaded-glass light fixtures, chrome-plated fountain spigots, and old-time lunch counter make you feel as though you've stepped right into a Hollywood vision of what a small-town ice-cream parlor should be. But, wonder of wonders, instead of some designer reproduction, it's the rare genuine article.

★ ★

Even rarer still, the ice-cream parlor is run by the same couple who were serving up vanilla phosphate and grilled cheese just after World War II. Thelma Nopoulos started washing dishes at the soda fountain when she was only ten years old, but she and George didn't marry until 1949. Their fathers, both Greek immigrants, couldn't help but play matchmakers, but it wasn't until after George returned from service overseas that "sparks began to fly behind the soda fountain." Thelma is now the charming hostess who'll step from behind the counter to chat about anything from local history (she published a book on Wilton history) to politics.

And, more than sixty years later, magic is still happening behind that very same soda fountain. What kind of magic, you dare ask? Just for starters, they've got Black Cows and Green Rivers on the menu. Never heard of them? Well, the Wilton Candy Kitchen is a veritable living museum of long-forgotten concoctions sure to make you swoon. How about a strawberry phosphate or a cherry Coke? Or, if you're feeling more daring, why not order a Pink Lady (strawberry, cherry, and vanilla flavorings), a Hadacol (root beer and cola), or a Dipsy Doodle (six different flavors mixed together).

Each and every concoction is made from water carbonated on the premises, syrup, and George's very own homemade ice cream. The place is so authentic, politicians have taken to stopping by on their forays through eastern Iowa in hopes that some of the Nopoulos charm will rub off on them. But don't let that deter you from visiting —the politicians never stick around for long. And, ever conscious of image, they never dare get caught on camera with a Pink Lady or Dipsy Doodle, so there'll be plenty left over for you and a sweetheart.

The Wilton Candy Kitchen is located at 310 Cedar Street in down-town Wilton, just south of US 6, midway between Iowa City and Davenport; the telephone number is (563) 732-2278. It's still open seven days a week, as it has been ever since 1910.

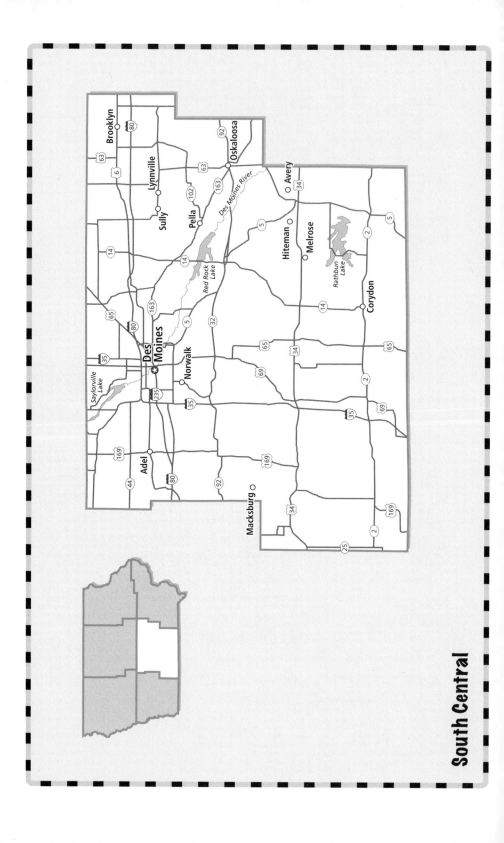

South Central

3

South Central

There's a strange *trend afoot in rural Iowa: Something in our state gains notoriety (usually thanks to Hollywood), and then not long after, someone decides to burn it down. It happened with South Central's bridges in Madison County after the Clint Eastwood movie came out and the tourists started coming. Covered bridges were going up in flames all over the place. And then, since the last edition of* Iowa Curiosities, *somebody lit the farmhouse featured in the movie on fire, so they don't offer tours there anymore, which means no more silly pictures of people lying in the claw-footed tub. (Up in North Central's Laurens, someone else put a match to the house once owned by Alvin Straight, the real-life central character in David Lynch's film* The Straight Story.) *It's enough to make you thankful for your total obscurity.*

If you want to learn a little self-defense just to be safe, start practicing your skillet throwing and then head to Macksburg to compete in the national championships. Or you can go check out the puny park in Hiteman, a bank that Jesse James robbed in Corydon (funny that hasn't been burnt down), and a mule cemetery in Oskaloosa.

One final sad loss to report: The Iowa State Museum had no idea what happened to the medical marvels display of objects removed from people's windpipes. There was a lot of chicken bones and what looked to be lint in the collection, but some neat shiny stuff, too, like pennies and safety pins. I miss it.

★ ★

Please Pass the Five Tons of Sweet Corn
Adel

"Corn's tricky," says Steve Amundsen of Moline, Illinois. "One person's fully eaten ear isn't the same as another person's fully eaten ear." Forgive him for waxing philosophical, but Amundsen was caught up in the excitement of watching a round of competition in the Corn Eating Contest at Adel's Sweet Corn Festival, held each summer on the second Saturday in August. And really, you couldn't help but agree he had a point. Even to an observer not inclined to philosophy, it was clear that some corn eaters were being a bit more conscientious about clearing the cob than others. (A few participants chomping their way through their allotment of ears seemed to be doing more corn spreading than a John Deere in springtime.) "It's not like a hot-dog-eating contest," Steve mused. "A hot dog is eaten, or it isn't. But corn on the cob is a whole nother story."

Rather than get caught up in the nearly impossible technicalities of fairly judging a corn-eating contest, though, we decided to join the estimated 10,000 other festival gorgers, I mean *goers,* for a few pieces of the more than five tons of Deardorf sweet corn served up—with healthy dollops of butter and loads of napkins—on Adel's beautiful town square. Dominated by a 1902 château-style county courthouse, Adel's square is where the whole festival unfolds: Vendors sell food and crafts on the sidewalks, bands and dance groups perform on the Court House Square Stage, townspeople and out-of-towners mix in the beer garden and dance in the square streets until midnight, and, of course, eaters with a competitive streak buzz through more than their fair share of Iowa's favorite crop.

Just a word of caution, though: It might be wise to steer clear of the Raccoon Valley Bank parking lot the Friday night before the Sweet Corn Festival. That's where the shucking takes place, and, no surprise here, with 10,000 pounds of corn to husk, they're always looking for enthusiastic volunteers. In lieu of those, however, any warm body will do.

Adel is located on US 169 north of I-80. The Sweet Corn Festival takes place the second Saturday in August, right on the courthouse square. For more information, call (515) 993-5472.

A Do-It-Yourself Tomb
Avery

The three unmarked pyramids sitting at the edge of Hickory Grove Cemetery aren't really in the best of shape. Mere septuagenarians, with the biggest of the trio standing only as tall as the rim of a basketball hoop, they still resemble their famous brethren in Egypt in at least one important way: They're ruins.

The lesson here? Leave the tomb building to the professionals.

★ ★

Built from local sandstone and concrete back in 1939, the pyramids (especially the largest one) are cracked all over and have little patches of concrete missing in places, giving them a sad, abandoned look in a place that already registers pretty high on the look-of-abandonment scale: a very rural cemetery in Iowa. But what they lack in beauty they more than make up for in mystery.

According to area historians, the pyramids were built by a man named Axel Peterson, a local gadfly and publisher of a little newspaper called the *Boomer,* a forum wherein he freely expressed his dissatisfactions with faraway politicians and next-door neighbors alike. The two smaller pyramids Peterson built as freestanding monuments (to himself, we imagine), according to local historian Helen Mathias, but the largest one he reportedly built as a burial crypt for himself and best friend Anton Heymooler.

Peterson used the bed of an old dump truck in the construction of the roof and walls of the vault and then poured two concrete benches, one for himself and one for Anton, so that they could rest in peace together for all eternity. And that explains the sad state of the pyramids themselves: This was, as they say pejoratively in the real estate business, a brother-in-law sort of project.

Neither Peterson nor Heymooler were ever buried in the crypt— Peterson was supposedly buried in a cemetery just east of Avery, and Heymooler was put to rest somewhere outside the county entirely— but whether it was because the crypt wasn't up to code or some other reason, no one seems to know for sure. What's the rule on dump truck recycling in burial vault construction anyway?

To find Hickory Grove Cemetery (also known as Covenanter Cemetery), follow 700th Avenue north out of Avery about 1 mile and take a left onto 160th Street. Follow 160th Street all the way to the T intersection, take a right onto 695th Street, and travel about a mile to where the road bends sharply to the right. Instead of following the road right, continue straight about 100 yards to the cemetery entrance on the left.

★ ★

Is This the United Nations? Nope, It's Iowa
Brooklyn

Not every small town in rural America raises the flag of the United Nations—a baby blue globe perched atop laurels against a field of white—but tiny Brooklyn did, and the residents didn't stop there. Ireland's green, white, and gold hang in front of the offices of the town rag, the *Brooklyn Chronicle*; the Union Jack stirs in the breeze just outside the door of Osborne Real Estate and Insurance; and a green and red flag with a shield in the center that we've yet to positively identify graces the pole in front of the local watering hole, the Front Street Tap. You don't have to look hard to find Italy, France, Germany, and Australia, too, among some of the more esoteric flags, all lined up as if waiting for an Olympic parade to roll through Brooklyn's sleepy redbrick downtown.

The brain-seed of Alex Whorley, a transplanted New York businessman looking for a way to wave customers off I-80 into Brooklyn's struggling downtown, the flags are paid for not by tax dollars, but through sales. In the dead center of town is a shop selling flags and memorabilia, as well as local knickknacks on consignment. Staffed by volunteers, the store's proceeds support the maintenance and replacement of all the flags, including a monstrous 20-by-38-foot Old Glory, flanked by flags from all fifty states, which flies day and night, rain or shine, atop an 80-foot pole behind the volunteer fire department.

And Mr. Whorley's civic boosterism didn't stop there. When the bridge over Big Bear Creek needed replacing, he had the good sense to try to sell the old Brooklyn (Iowa) Bridge on eBay. Reportedly a woman offered the town $50,000 for its Brooklyn Bridge, but no one could figure out a way to move it, so instead of making a profit, they had to pay to have it torn down.

The flags are no gimmick, though, and the town seems truly proud to fly the colors of so many nations. Now if we could just figure out where all those nations are on the map, we might feel as

Anyone up for playing Guess That Flag? Catherine Cole

cosmopolitan in Brooklyn, Iowa, as the denizens of that other Brooklyn surely do.

Brooklyn is located just off I-80, midway between Des Moines and Iowa City, at mile marker 197.

A Toast to the Time We Got Robbed

Corydon

If you want some proof that time heals all wounds, allow us to offer exhibit A: Corydon's Jesse James Days, held each year on the first Friday and Saturday in June. The celebration, which includes the three big Bs of Iowa festivaldom—beer garden, bands, and barbecued meats—is held to commemorate the robbing of Corydon's Ocobock Bank of somewhere between $6,000 and $10,000, depending on whom you ask. And, in case you hadn't guessed, the festival is called Jesse James Days because Jesse James, along with his brother Frank, Cole Younger, and Clell Miller, did the robbing.

A few days before an important town meeting, Jesse and his gang arrived in town posing as cattle buyers, apparently the modern-day equivalent of traveling salesmen. The day of the meeting, on June 3, 1871, most of the townspeople were gathered at the Methodist church, so the four outlaws attracted little notice as they rode into town on horseback dressed in linen dusters.

The gang found the Ocobock Bank tended by a single lonely clerk and forced him to open the safe with either the old "Got change for a hundred-dollar bill?" trick or the old "You've got a gun in your face—open the vault now" trick, historians aren't sure which. At any rate, Jesse and his gang made off with somewhere around $8,000 (give or take $2,000) of the townspeople's money. Legend even has it that the gang was so disappointed by how easy the heist was that they showed up at the town meeting to taunt the crowd with the fact that they had just robbed their bank. At first everyone thought it was a hoax, but when word came from the clerk that the bank had indeed been robbed, citizens formed a posse and pursued the James gang all the way to Missouri before losing the trail.

And now, 138 years and a lot of water under the bridge later, Corydon celebrates the day it was an easy target to a famous outlaw. If you happen to miss the celebration, you can still get your Jesse James fix at the Prairie Trails Museum, where there is a display of the

★ ★

actual safe that James robbed inside a re-creation of Ocobock Bank, as well as various other James artifacts.

The lesson here? You know something's history when it no longer stings. So raise a glass with Corydon citizens in honor of getting the shakedown and then having it rubbed in your face.

In June, July, and August, the Prairie Trails Museum, located on IA 2 in Corydon, is open Monday through Saturday from 10:00 a.m. to 5:00 p.m. and Sunday 1:00 to 5:00 p.m. In April, May, September, and October, the museum is open daily from 1:00 to 5:00 p.m. For more information, call (641) 872-2211. The Ocobock Bank was located on the square where Citizens Bank now stands. The eastern exterior wall of the bank is affixed with a plaque marking the historic site.

A Bike Ride through the Country with 20,000 Friends
Des Moines

In 1973, the first year the *Des Moines Register* sponsored a bicycle ride across the entire state of Iowa, 300 people showed up for the start, and a total of 114 riders made the entire distance. (Did the rest give up when they found the state wasn't as flat as they imagined?) Thirty-six years later, the *Register*'s Annual Great Bicycle Ride Across Iowa (RAGBRAI, pronounced *rag-bry*) is now the oldest, longest, largest, and possibly best-fed bicycle-touring event in the world (you didn't think Iowans would bike all day without the promise of pork for dinner, did you?), so popular that officials now limit the number of weeklong participants to 8,500 to maintain a semblance of sanity. With day-trippers joining in around urban centers like Des Moines, the pedaling, Lycra-clad ranks can swell to five figures: An estimated 23,000 bikers rode from Boone to Des Moines during RAGBRAI XVI, a group that, were they to incorporate themselves as a town (how about Saddlesoreville for a name?), would be about the twenty-seventh largest in the state.

The ride began as a kind of challenge between *Des Moines Register* writers (and avid cyclists) John Karras and Don Kaul. Karras suggested to Kaul that he ride his bike across Iowa and write columns about his experiences along the way. Kaul told Karras he would do it but on one condition: that Karras ride with him. Karras, of course, agreed. They got approval from the paper's managing editor, offered an invitation to *Register* readers to join them on the trip (only six weeks before they were scheduled to set out), and RAGBRAI was born.

One of the more eccentric participants that first year was Clarence Pickard, an eighty-three-year-old from Indianola. His touring bicycle of choice? A used ladies' Schwinn. His workout gear to keep comfortable in the late-August heat? Long woolen underwear, long pants, a long-sleeved shirt, and a silver pith helmet. Pickard completed the entire ride, including the 110-mile leg from Des Moines to Williamsburg, in 100-degree-plus heat, and became a favorite with readers.

A mixture of town parade, big block party, and endurance test, RAGBRAI is essentially a different bike ride every summer. Each year ride planners lay out the west-to-east route to pass through different towns; by its thirty-sixth in 2008, RAGBRAI had passed through all 99 Iowa counties and 780 Iowa towns. Though the variety is surely appreciated by return participants, there may have been another factor: As hospitable as Iowans are, a crowd of 8,500 hungry, thirsty bikers returning every July—filling the hotels, restaurants, bars, bathrooms, campgrounds, bedrooms, and lawns—might be too much for even the most welcoming Iowa town to handle.

For information and registration, go to www.ragbrai.org or call (800) 474-3342.

Head-on Joe's Show
Des Moines

Joseph "Head-on Joe" Connolly couldn't take credit for coming up with the idea of running two train engines straight into each other at high speeds for the edification and entertainment of large paying

crowds. (But then again, coming up with an idea like that is a dubious distinction.) That honor falls to a Mr. William Crush, vice president of the Missouri, Kansas, and Texas Railroad, who dreamed up a rather dramatic way of putting to rest his company's old locomotives while making some money at the same time. In 1896 the appropriately named Mr. Crush staged his first, and last, head-on locomotive collision for a group of paying customers in Missouri, among them one Joseph Connolly. The end result? A terrific crash (as expected), an extremely large double-boiler explosion (unexpected), and two spectators dead and many more wounded.

Joseph Connolly might have come away from the event an anti–train wreck activist. Instead, he brought head-on train-wreck madness to the Iowa State Fair. The first Iowa State Fair train wreck was staged in 1897, the second in 1921, and the third and final one in 1932, which drew more than 35,000 spectators.

This last wreck, reportedly the most dramatic, was a head-on collision between the Roosevelt and the Hoover. (Hoover was battling Roosevelt to hold onto his presidency at the time.) According to Floyd Deets, superintendent of the fairgrounds from the 1940s until 1985 and a firsthand observer of the 1932 crash, workers removed the seats from the coaches, loaded the front of the locomotives with dynamite, and set tanks of kerosene inside so that the trains would explode and burst into towering flames upon impact. "There was a challenge as to which engineer would jump out last," he said. "But since one was going downhill at a pretty good clip, and the other was working pretty hard to go uphill, the engineer going down must have had to jump earlier."

The trains crashed, both Roosevelt and Hoover went down in flames, and the mild-mannered Midwesterners loved it. Joseph Connolly might not have come up with the idea himself, but he sure knew good, clean, catastrophic fair-time fun when he saw it.

★ ★

The Iowa State Fairgrounds Museum displays a bell from the 1932 train, as well as photographs of the wreck. But alas, they no longer stage wrecks. Take I-80 to exit 141 (US 65), and then take US 65 south to exit 79. Follow University Avenue west to the fairgrounds. For more information about the fair, call (800) 545-3247 or visit www.iowastatefair.org.

A Skywalk with 18 Holes
Des Moines

Des Moines isn't the only Midwestern city with skywalks to protect citizens from the fickle weather. But it may be the only city to host a three-course, 18-hole miniature golf tournament 20 feet above its streets.

Des Moines has more than 3 miles of skywalks downtown, where the Principal Charity Classic hosts the Skywalk Open the first weekend in February. More than 1,800 people put their skills to the test on a total of four different 18-hole courses each year, making it the largest indoor golf tournament in the world. Local businesses and community groups sponsor individual holes, and participants compete in one of three divisions—singles, doubles, or foursomes—with prizes going to the top three finishers in each division.

In its twenty-four years of existence, the tournament has gotten a lot of good press: *Midwest Living* called it "one of the best wintertime celebrations," and Festivals.com included it in its list of Greatest Events on Earth.

Though we're sure course officials have things under control, may we suggest some rules for the tournament? Recarpet all divots, no mulligans for balls lost under the heat registers, and no banging one's head against the skywalk glass upon missing a putt for birdie. It leaves smudge marks.

The Skywalk Open is held each year the first weekend in February. Visit www.skywalkgolf.com for more information.

★ ★

Puny Park
Hiteman

Hiteman is one of those towns carrying the warning that if you blink, you'll miss it. The list of what it doesn't have includes the small-town standards—a gas station, a bar, and a church. Hiteman doesn't even have a downtown to speak of, but it does have 101 residents and a claim to fame: Iowa's smallest park.

A park with picnic space for two. Clint Buckner

★ ★

Keep your eyes wide open as you head into "town"; turn south on Fourth Street and there it is, up ahead, where the gravel road splits into a Y, a roughly 10-by-20-foot plot of grass. Technically, it's just big enough to hold the entire town, but that's not saying all that much. A wedding was once held there, but the couple was presumed to be on a tiny budget.

The hand pump in the center of the park is the reason it exists. The pump dates back to the time when Hiteman was an active mining town and there were wells, spaced a block or so apart, that made up the public water supply. The use of wells stopped in the 1950s, though the one in what is now the park remained. When past residents came to visit, they took photos of the remaining pump for nostalgia's sake, so someone thought it would be nice to pretty it up with a paint job. Then Howard Thomas, who lives a few steps away from the park with his wife, Lois, stuck a bench near the pump. A park was born.

Over the years a flagpole flying the state and national flag was added. During the town's centennial in 1990, the Thomases' daughter made a sign, now mounted to the flagpole, that reads CITY PARK, HITEMAN, IOWA. The couple has taken over park landscaping as well. Lois added some plastic flowers in a pail (she says that real ones don't grow so well here), and Howard walks around the park every once in a while with a weed wacker, as the park is not big enough to hold a mower.

Once people noticed the park was shrinking, due to graters and tractors traveling the gravel roads surrounding it, Howard and some other neighborhood men got some bridge planks from the county and edged the park in. This act of conservation ensures Hiteman's claim to fame remains an attraction—for those who don't blink and then miss it.

Traveling south from Des Moines on IA 5, turn west on 170th Street into Hiteman. Go south on Fourth Street, and you'll see the park straight ahead.

Invasion of the Dolls
Lynnville

Norma Conover took up doll making as therapy when she was diag-
nosed with cancer back in 1979. She and husband Bruce made their
first doll in 1980, poured their first ceramic molds, and started teaching doll-making classes in 1985. Now, twenty-nine years and more
than 600 dolls later, the Conovers haven't got much room left in the
farmhouse for themselves, let alone their visiting kids and grandkids.
And while the doll making may have helped Norma win her battle
with cancer, now she's got a different, though much less pressing,
challenge—how to stop making them. "You know what hobbies
tend to do," Norma said. "They take over. Sometimes now we call it
a disease."

"We have dolls throughout the whole house," Norma told me at
the beginning of the tour, which proved a bit of an understatement.
It's as if the house has been invaded by an army of cheerful, orderly,
extremely well-dressed Victorian munchkins. And Norma and Bruce
made every single one of them.

The dolls come in various shapes and sizes, with outfits ranging from a black-velvet winter coat and fur muffler to a frilly pink
party dress. There are lots of pastel colors, of course, and pink pre-
dominates, probably because the majority of the dolls are girls. The
most fascinating specimens are the "settings," or doll portraits, that
Norma's done of close family members. Working from a baby picture,
she finds a doll mold that closely approximates the appearance of the
child, makes the doll, and then dresses it up to look exactly like the
baby in the picture. Then she displays the doll right beside the picture
and, voilà, she has a baby portrait filled with stuffing of someone
dear to her heart. She's done one of her husband, her mother, her
aunt, her granddaughters, her two sisters, and even one of herself.

The Conovers have deep roots in Lynnville. Bruce's great-
grandparents homesteaded the land back in 1853 and lived in a log
cabin for seventeen years before building the farmhouse where the

That's a lot of unblinking eyes in one room.

Conovers now house their dolls. And one of the fringe benefits of the Dollyville tour is that you get a thumbnail history of an original Iowa settler family and farmhouse along the way. If great-grandpa could only see his bedroom now.

Visits are by appointment only; call (641) 594-3449.

Flying Skillets
Macksburg

The Macksburg National Skillet Throwing Contest started in the mid-1970s, and even though Kevin Jackson is one of fifteen Macksburg residents who plan the thing, he has no idea how it began. One can only imagine how throwing an iron skillet at a scarecrow for sport started, or why it took off as it did, but Kevin says that today's competition draws up to sixty teams of five. That's more than double the town's population of 140.

The idea is to throw the skillet at a set of three scarecrows, each with a piece of plastic-tile pipe for a neck. A basketball rests on the

★ ★

pipe. Contestants are awarded points for knocking the basketball off the pipe—5 points for a clean hit, square at the ball, and 1 point for anything that removes the basketball without hitting it directly. Underhand is the preferred throwing style, though some contestants mix it up with sidearm or overhand lobs. There's a three-sided cage around the scarecrows ever since two unfortunate competitors were hit with flying skillets a few years back—clean hits, by the way.

Sponsored teams come from Macksburg and neighboring towns. Kevin says there are even some annually returning teams from "down south" (Iowa, that is) as well as Colorado and beyond. Once a group from Japan happened upon the contest and entered. "They was real nice people, but they wasn't real big and just not strong enough," Kevin reports.

A festival is built around the contest, which includes a parade, a flea market, food vendors, and, for the kids, a pedal-tractor pull and a greased pig contest. Another draw: Chicken Bingo, where you pay a dollar to put your name on one of sixty-four spots on a piece of plywood. A chicken is let loose on the plywood, and if it poops on your name, you win half the pot. A sweet victory, yes, but not nearly as sweet as winning the celebration's most sought-after title: Skillet Throwing Champion of America.

The Macksburg Festival's National Skillet Throwing Contest takes place each June on the Saturday before Father's Day. To get to Macksburg, take I-80 west of Des Moines to IA 169 south, then turn west on CR G61 just south of Winterset. For more information, call Kevin at (641) 768-2291.

A Little Town with a Lot of Irish
Melrose

Want to kiss the Blarney Stone but only have time and cash for a day trip to, say, southern Iowa? Well, you've got the luck of the Irish on your side. There just so happens to be a piece of the Blarney

★ ★

Stone—the rock high in the battlements of Blarney castle that sup-
posedly gives all who kiss it the "gift of the gab"—in the little town
of Melrose, founded by Irish immigrants in 1882.

Of course, the authenticity of the stone has never been verified by
outside sources, and Melrose citizens most certainly inherited the Irish
penchant for stretching the truth. Townspeople even claim that Melrose's own BLARNEY STONE, as it's inscribed, was brought to Iowa from
Ireland by leprechauns during the potato famine. Likely story. Who
were these leprechauns? What proof of their existence can Melrose
offer? Death certificates, tax records, vintage emerald-green clothes
in extremely small sizes? The story sounds good, but we want some
hard evidence before planting our lips against any strange stones.

Melrose has always been Irish, but downtown renovations have
made the place look as Irish as its founders surely did. When their
downtown of seven or eight buildings threatened to topple over,
the whole town banded together, scared away the raccoons, hauled
away tons of debris, rewired, reroofed, and then painted the exteri-
ors using color schemes common on the Emerald Isle. As a finishing
touch, volunteers made flower boxes adorned with shamrocks and
hung them on the front of every building. They even placed leprechaun statues at strategic locations. The end result is a charming
Main Street that highlights the town's heritage.

If you want more proof that the blood runs green in the veins of
Melrose citizens, you need look no farther than the street signs. Every
street name has something to do with Ireland: They've got Shamrock
Street, Leprechaun Lane, Cork Street, Tralee Street, and Kells Avenue,
to name just a few. And Melrose has the only town park in the
state with a Gaelic name, Tolendol Park. (*Tolendol* means "meeting
place.") With so much Irish around, it almost feels like sacrilege to
doubt the authenticity of Melrose's Blarney Stone.

Melrose is located on IA 68, just south of US 34. For more information about the town, call (641) 932-5108.

★ ★

Norwalk's Superstar Twirling Coach
Norwalk

If you want to talk elite baton twirlers in Iowa, you're talking about a serious legacy—Jan Stivers's legacy, that is. The fifty-eight-year-old Norwalk native and owner of Norwalk Superstars Baton, Dance, and Gymnastics Center has coached an awe-inspiring number of girls who've gone on to become Iowa State, University of Northern Iowa, and University of Iowa twirlers, many of them receiving scholarships for their amazing abilities with the baton. (The University of Iowa and the University of Hawaii are the only two universities in the country offering full financial aid to their baton twirlers.) And more of Jan Stivers's incredibly talented twirlers are sure to come.

In case you haven't been to an Iowa State, University of Northern Iowa, or University of Iowa football game (you're not from around these parts, are you?), baton at the collegiate level is not the run-of-the-mill twirling you remember from childhood. A college twirler performs a set routine for each song the marching band plays during halftime and postgame shows, moving her way around the football field in a dramatic solo performance that is part dance, part gymnastics, and part baton twirling. Perhaps the most impressive moments come with the astoundingly high baton tosses: Stivers-trained twirlers regularly throw the baton 30, 40, 50 feet in the air, perform an elegant acrobatic feat while it flashes silver through the fall sky, and then gracefully catch the baton just before it embeds itself in the turf. Some twirlers toss two or three batons at the same time; Julie Canterbury—World Champion Twirler, former University of Iowa Golden Girl, and one-time Stivers student—could even twirl a baton around her neck. Golden Girl performances are so mesmerizing that they can make the happenings on the gridiron pale a little in comparison.

So what's the secret to Jan's coaching success? Her main ingredients, she says, are lots of positive reinforcement and lots of fun. "I try hard to make practice as fun as I can. I'll have them twirl and toss water balloons, or make up silly games," she says. Stivers not only teaches the girls different twirling techniques and moves, but also models for her students from a very young age how to artfully choreograph their own performances. "I ask them, 'What is this music telling you to do here?' and they begin to learn that, say, a crescendo is telling them to do something spectacular." As for the many moves she has dreamt up for her girls, she says, "You never know what's going to come out of my head. I never know what's going to come out of my head. I've come up with some crazy ideas." Like twirling piano keys or animal bones, for starters.

And she never seems to tire of finding fresh ideas. Not long ago she went out to dinner with a group of twirling judges, and the women started demonstrating tricks with dinner knives. "We were a bunch of women twirling knives for each other, saying, 'Hey, have you seen this trick? What about this one?' Luckily, we were in a room that didn't have many people in it, so we didn't scare anybody off."

The most important ingredients in Jan's success might just be an almost palpable passion for twirling and an even more palpable love for her girls. "I've been twirling for over fifty years. I still love it, I love the girls, and I'm still learning new things," Jan says. And she's still single-handedly supplying the state of Iowa with its yearly requirement of phenomenally talented collegiate twirlers.

Norwalk is located on IA 28 about 12 miles south of Des Moines, east of I-35 (exit 65). Norwalk Superstars Baton, Dance, and Gymnastics Center is just south of town off IA 28 at 360 Wright Road. For information about classes, call (515) 981-4298.

The Eccentric Millionaire of Mahaska County
Oskaloosa

George Daily lived in a dilapidated house across the street from Oskaloosa High School; shuffled around town in dirty, rumpled clothes; talked to almost no one; and spent his days reading the *Wall Street Journal* in the town's library, playing checkers on a park bench in the

★ ★

George gave Oskaloosa a big gift that keeps on giving.

central square, and scouring trash bins for rags, cardboard, and old tires. (In other words, he was a little eccentric, even for an Iowan.) He was, some people claim, Oskaloosa's own Boo Radley, the recluse in Harper Lee's novel *To Kill a Mockingbird*. Some students were afraid of him and claimed that the old man would grab kids and they'd never be seen again.

Now, thanks in part to Daily's generosity, high school students attend classes in a new building that adjoins a state-of-the art, 695-seat performing arts center, George Daily Auditorium. (A bronze statue of Daily playing checkers sits out front of the auditorium.) The students have new cheerleading uniforms, new computers in their English classes, new dugouts at the baseball field. One young man even got $25 to put toward guitar lessons.

When Daily died in 1993 at the age of eighty-four, he left a con-siderable sum of money—money few people in town dreamed he

★ ★

ever had—in trust for the benefit of Oskaloosa. How much money? More than $6 million, all from oil revenues generated on a small parcel of land his itinerant laborer father bought in Ascension Parish, Louisiana, back in the 1920s. Now, sixteen years after his death, his trust has helped pay for hundreds of community projects all over town, from a new park—the old Daily home was torn down and turned into a community wildflower garden—to a summer-theater camp for kids. Daily's trust is still worth millions, and trustees accept applications for grants year-round. Local groups applying for aid must pay for a portion of their projects themselves, however, because the fund is designed not to bankroll ideas outright, but to jumpstart cooperative community initiatives.

As of yet, there's no talk of changing Oskaloosa's name to Dailyville, but who knows? Six-million-dollar gifts can make people feel pretty darn grateful.

The George Daily Auditorium is located next to the high School at 1800 North Third Street. From downtown take US 63 north to O Avenue. Take a right onto O Avenue and then a left onto North Third Street. The auditorium will be on the right. For more information about tickets and performances, call (641) 672-0799.

May She Be Stubborn in Peace
Oskaloosa

You've probably heard of a pet cemetery, a final resting place for Fifi and Fido, but what about a mule cemetery? (Sounds a little exclusive doesn't it? Why not let cows, hogs, and horses in, too?) Nelson Pioneer Farm, located just a few miles north of Oskaloosa on US 63, has what appears to be the state's only all-mule cemetery. You can't buy your favorite beast of burden a burial plot here, though, for at least two reasons: (1) The cemetery is a historic site, and (2) since two mules are already interred on the rather cramped 15-by-15-foot grounds, bordered by a small white picket fence, there's no room left for any other dearly departed hybrids.

HERE LIES
'BECKY'
FAITHFUL
WHITE MULE
THAT SERVED
IN UNITED STATES
ARTILLERY
IN CIVIL WAR
DIED MARCH 1888
AGE 34 YEARS
OWNED BY
DANIEL NELSON

Our dearly departed beasts of burden.

Nelson Pioneer Farm is a collection of fifteen historic buildings, including a schoolhouse, a log cabin, a post office, and a Quaker meetinghouse, located on beautiful grounds a few miles north of Oskaloosa. The heart of the complex is the Nelson homestead, with its antebellum farmhouse and barn and, of course, its mule cemetery. Both graves are marked by a simple rectangular wooden plaque painted white and rounded at the top corners to look like a gravestone. "Here lies 'Jennie,'" one reads. "Famous white mule that served in the Civil War. Branded us. Died March 1891 age 42 years. Owned by Daniel Nelson."

Becky, the only other mule buried in the cemetery (her name is in quotation marks on her grave marker, too—maybe the names were aliases?), was a white-haired Union artillery mule that lived to be thirty-four.

A Civil War veteran himself, Daniel Nelson obviously felt indebted enough to his trusty white mules to mark out a prime final resting place for them. Whatever their relationship was like, one thing is sure: War brings men and their mules together in ways that cannot be explained.

The Nelson Pioneer Farm is open from mid-May to mid-October. Hours of operation are Tuesday through Saturday from 10:00 a.m. to 4:30 p.m. and Sunday 1:00 to 4:30 p.m. Take US 63 north out of Oskaloosa to CR T65 and follow the signs to the Pioneer Farm at 2294 Oxford Avenue. Call (641) 672-2989 for more information.

A Big Dutch Windmill in Iowa
Pella

Even if you're from Scranton or Hong Kong, you may already know Pella for its eponymous corporation, Pella Windows, the company headquartered in town that manufacturers high-quality windows. If you've never been to Pella, though, you're in for an ethnic surprise. A Dutch immigrant community founded by a small band of Hollanders in 1847, Pella has held tightly to its old-world heritage, especially

Which tastes better, Dutch- or Danish-milled flour?

downtown, with its colorful, European-style storefronts, authentic Dutch bakery, and towering Dutch windmill just east of the town square. The end result is like seeing a Midwestern gal dressed up in Dutch costume—a pretty sight, but you can't help but wonder if she wouldn't feel a little more comfortable in jeans and a T-shirt.

The Dutch windmill, officially known as the Vermeer Mill and Interpretive Center, is part of Pella's Historical Village, a collection of twenty-one historic buildings, including a log cabin, a blacksmith shop, a church, and the boyhood home of Pella's own little outlaw Wyatt Earp, who lived here until he was fifteen. Completed in July 2002, the 90-foot-tall windmill (with an impressive height of almost 124 feet when you measure all the way to the tip of the most upright blade) is the tallest working windmill in the United States. (Since the mill is in the heart of downtown Pella, it had to be built taller than surrounding buildings to catch the wind.) An international effort, the windmill was built by a man from the Netherlands and then assembled on-site by two craftsmen from Holland.

Village employees operate the mill, grinding wheat into flour that's used by local restaurants and bakeries. If you want to make your own extremely authentic Dutch pastries, you can buy some of the mill's flour, tied up in an attractive souvenir bag, at the Historical Village's gift shop.

The Historical Village is home to not only the tallest working Dutch windmill in the United States, but also the smallest Dutch village. Be sure to check out the 1:24 scale Miniature Dutch Village, featuring eighty very small, steep-roofed Dutch buildings (some of which are elaborately furnished), a water-filled canal, a working train, and a whole lot of $\frac{1}{24}$-sized Hollanders dressed in very small but still quite authentic Dutch costumes.

Pella Historical Village is located east of the town square at 507 Franklin Street. (Just walk toward the 90-foot-tall windmill.) It's open from mid-March through December, Monday through Saturday from 9:00 a.m. to 4:00 p.m. For more information, call (641) 628-4311 or visit www.pellatuliptime.com/historical-village.

★ ★

Wagon Wheel Art
Sully

At the age of eighty-seven, Leonard Maasdam—Iowa sorghum farmer, builder, and inventor—erected a 60-foot-tall sculpture made out of more than 200 steel wagon wheels on land he owned just north of Sully. The towering sculpture is an impressive accomplishment for anyone, let alone an octogenarian, but if the whole truth be known, Leonard had a little help from his friends. "He was putting together those old steel wheels," his grandson Craig Maasdam told me, "and I'd come out at night and start looking at his welds. And some weren't very good; they were coming apart, and so I'd spend two, three, four hours fixing 'em each night." And, apparently, Leonard never knew.

According to his grandson, the sculpture was "kind of a last hur-rah" for a man whose life was filled with tinkering, building, and inventing. Among his many accomplishments, Leonard Maasdam

Taking wagon wheel art to new heights.

built a sorghum mill (located a few miles down the road from the wagon-wheel tree) out of parts salvaged from scrap yards as far away as Chicago, invented a trenching machine with Gary Vermeer (called the Vermeer Trencher) used for laying tile in farm fields to improve drainage, helped perfect something called the Pella Irrigation System, and built two underground round houses just north of Pella that can be heated and cooled with mind-boggling efficiency.

Leonard's first passion was sorghum farming, though, and his recycled-parts sorghum mill—he even made use of the back end of an old car—is now the largest operating sorghum mill in the United States and possibly the world. In case you're like me and don't quite know what sorghum is, it's a sweet syrup made from the juice of the sorghum plant. Don't confuse it with molasses, though. As Craig Maasdam told me, "Molasses is just the junk that's left over after they refine sugar from sugar cane." Leonard's daughter, son-in-law, and grandson Craig now run the mill and produce more sorghum than anyone in the world.

Leonard got the idea for a sculpture made out of wagon wheels during one of his many trips to Wisconsin delivering sorghum. "It was different from the one he built," said Craig, "not nearly as big and a whole different shape, but that's where he got the idea." But, apparently, Leonard didn't get caught up in technicalities when talking about his creation. "He just said he came up with the idea himself. But I know he saw one in Wisconsin because he showed me the postcard of the thing."

L. J. Maasdam died in April 2003 at the age of ninety-eight. "He didn't do much after that wagon-wheel tree," Craig said, with a hint of sadness in his voice. But as far as last hurrahs go, it sure is a doozy.

Mr. Maasdam's sculpture is located 3 miles south of exit 179 on I-80. Head south on CR T38 to Bethel Cemetery, then turn right at the cemetery and head west. You'll see the sculpture straight ahead. There's a small parking area for visitors by the picnic table. In September the family offers tours of Leonard's sorghum mill down the road. Call (641) 594-4376 for information.

America's Sweetest War

The year was 1839. An unidentified Missourian cut down three trees occupied by honey-producing bees in a small corner of a disputed border territory—now in the southern part of Van Buren County and the northern part of Missouri's Clark County—laid claim to by both Missouri and Iowa. Iowa tried the honey thief in absentia and fined him a whopping $1.50.

Missouri had become the second of the Louisiana Purchase territories (after Louisiana) to achieve statehood in 1821, and Iowa was soon to become a state, so the question of the legal boundary between the two was a pressing issue. In 1838 a federal surveyor had laid out four possible boundaries, each of which represented a different reading of historical data (what a troublemaker). The distance between the surveyor's northernmost and southernmost boundaries was about 10 miles, creating a 10-mile strip of no-state's land all the way from the Des Moines River west to the Missouri River, totaling some 2,600 square miles.

Angry over the honey tree incident, Missouri governor Lilburn Boggs issued a proclamation stating that the surveyor's northernmost boundary was the legal state line, and in response Iowa governor Robert Lucas ordered the arrest of anyone trying to exercise authority in the disputed borderlands (what Boggs called "the seat of excitement"). At Governor Boggs's insistence, Missouri's Clark County sheriff Uriah Gregory went to collect taxes in present-day Van Buren County, but Iowans in the disputed territory took him into custody and held him in Burlington. (He was allowed to roam around town and enjoy the sights—apparently Gregory enjoyed his free Iowa vacation quite a bit.)

By December both sides began to arm (and we use the term loosely) for battle. Iowa's Governor Lucas predicted that the dispute "might ultimately lead to the effusion of blood," and called up 1,200 men. The Missourians tried to raise 2,200 militiamen, but only about half showed up—one of the "soldiers" that did make it came armed with a sausage stuffer. One militia company from Missouri's Lewis County brought six wagons of provisions, five of which were reportedly filled with booze.

Clark County sent a delegation to Iowa to work out a truce, and the militiamen spent two days camped out in the snow and the cold, drinking whiskey. In order to pass the time, they split a haunch of venison, labeled one side Governor Boggs and one side Governor Lucas, and shot each one full of holes. In Iowa the two sides agreed to allow the federal government to mediate the dispute and told their partying "troops" to go home. Ultimately, the two states came up with a brilliant solution—they'd split the disputed territory down the middle—and in 1850 they set boundary markers every 10 miles. Northern Iowans console themselves over the lost 5-mile strip of land running from one end of their state to another with a cruel joke: Handing over a part of southern Iowa to Missouri was mutually beneficial, because it raised the average IQ of both states.

You can visit the "seat of excitement" by traveling to the area between Mount Sterling and Farmington on CR J56, south of IA 2.

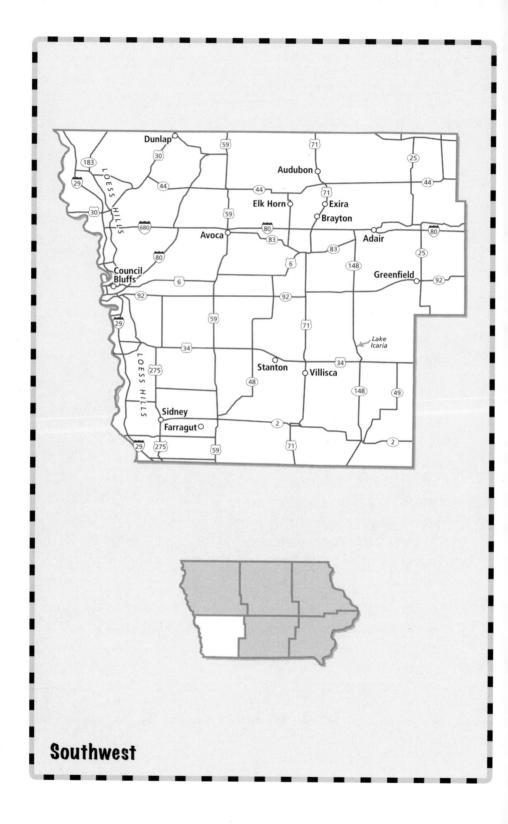

Southwest

4

Southwest

The Southwest is *the only region of the state that has dreams of going Western. There's a long cattle tradition here, and Albert, Audubon's 30-foot-tall concrete bull, definitely makes me want to head out on the range. Check out the 172-foot-long beef mural at Audubon's Nathaniel Hamlin Park for more evidence of Western dreams. And if that's not proof enough, little Sidney calls itself Rodeotown USA and is reported to have one of the biggest rodeos in the country. The historical museum there also has one of the most exquisite collections of dirt you'll ever see.*

Unfortunately, Council Bluff's oldest Dairy Queen in the country shut down, apparently making its last ice-cream stand in the summer of 2005. Maybe it was because they didn't have chocolate? And the lawnmower museum in Crescent shut down, too, and didn't leave a forwarding address.

But there are some great new additions, especially for those reluctant to leave their car. You can see a 16-foot-tall cutout painting of a girl holding a torn teddy bear and scolding her 8-foot-tall Dalmatian outside of Dunlap, a tree right in the middle of a road in Brayton, a Volkswagen Beetle turned into a giant spider in Avoca, and, in Greenfield, a boulder painted a different patriotic theme each year just in time to honor veterans on Memorial Day. None of it requires unbuckling your seatbelt.

Villisca's axe-murder house is still going strong, and now there's even a full-length documentary about it. And Stanton, the Little White City, is still pretty white. What did you expect? This is still Iowa, after all, no matter who we vote for.

★ ★

A Robbed Train and a Smiling Tower

Adair

Adair's most visible landmark is its water tower, a yellow beacon painted with a simple smiling face that's easily seen from I-80. Its other landmark requires you exit the interstate and keep your eyes peeled for a roadside gravel loop, which serves as the turnoff for a locomotive wheel bearing a plaque that reads, "Site of the first train robbery in the West, committed by the notorious Jesse James and his gang of outlaws July 21, 1873." Town literature also calls it the world's first robbery of a moving train.

Hollywood would have you think differently about that last claim. Michael Crichton's *The Great Train Robbery* was purported to be based on a true story about the world's first robbery of a moving

Even Jesse James needed to start somewhere. Clint Buckner

train—in England in 1855. And the folks in Verdi, Nevada, say they had a train robbery there back in 1870, before Adair's and even farther west.

Regardless, there definitely was a train robbery here in 1873, and to clarify, the train wasn't moving while it was robbed. The James Gang derailed the train, killing two people and injuring several others. Then two men (believed to be Jesse and Frank James) hopped on board the train, forced the guard to open the safe, and found $2,000—a full $73,000 short of what they were expecting. They gathered another $1,000 from passengers' pockets and then escaped.

At present, the site holds the wheel and plaque as well as a few feet of the original train tracks. From it you can see the town's other claim to fame, the smiley-face water tower—less historically significant, but definitely more straightforward and cheerful.

To get to the Jesse James train-robbery site, take exit 75 off I-80 and turn on CR G30. You'll see it on the left. For more information, contact the Adair County Conservation Board at (641) 743-6450.

No (Small) Bull
Audubon

You can see the bull from the highway. He's a giant Hereford with a giant set of baby blue eyes, a giant set of horns, and a giant set of, well, those reproductive components that separate the bulls from the cows.

Albert (as the bull is named) stands 30 feet tall, has a horn span of 15 feet, and weighs 45 tons. A promotion for Audubon's beef industry, he is the world's largest bull.

Albert's story springs from another industry promotion called Operation T-Bone, started in 1951. During the annual shipment of Audubon-area cattle to Chicago, shippers and local businessmen rode along in the train's drafty caboose—except for banker Albert Kruse, who said he'd refrain from the trip to the big city until there was a

★ ★

more comfortable traveling arrangement. Albert's wish was granted, and Operation T-Bone was born as a weeklong celebration culminating in the trip to Chicago, with the cattle in the cattle cars and the shippers and businessmen like Albert partying in style in a Pullman car. At present, Operation T-Bone is a one-day September festival with crafts and entertainment.

The big bull, erected in 1963, was named for this comfort-seeking businessman. The Jaycees took on the project, and raised about $30,000 to fund it. His steel frame, made from salvaged Iowa windmills, is covered in wire mesh, which is covered in three coats of concrete, which is covered in cement (for texture), which is covered in about 650 pounds of paint. Albert is promoted as being "authentic

By the looks of things, this bull should have courage to spare. Berit Thorkelson

right down to his toenails," and this brave and extremely detailed dedication to physical authenticity is certainly difficult to miss.

Albert the Bull is located off US 71 at the south edge of Audubon. For more information, call the Audubon Chamber of Commerce at (712) 563-3780.

The Prettiest Beef Mural You'll Ever See
Audubon

Come to Audubon's Nathaniel Hamlin Park for the eighteen antique windmills lined up like children's pinwheels along the hillside, the pair of elk in the side pasture, and the impressively authentic-looking rehabilitated Flintstones (the famously paradoxical modern Stone Age family) car. That way you can count the park's stunning beef mural as a 9-foot-tall, 172-foot-long agribusiness bonus.

A local artist named Cam Ross painted the mural, which offers an epic display of steak's long journey from the wide-open Texas range, on up through Iowa—for the less romantic confinement and meat-packing parts of the trip—all the way to some slightly creepy-looking family's dinner table in Anyplace USA. (Don't their eyes have that alien-abducted stare?) The mural is really stunning and weird in a 1970s sort of way, with towering and aggressively cheerful depictions of everything from cowboys (the Marlboro Man was used as a model for the cowpoke on the wide-open range), to long emerald rows of Iowa corn, to a train-on-tractor-trailer near-collision on I-80, all of it popping from the huge panels in better-than-life color.

Cam did the mural on commission in 1973 for the newly completed livestock-sale barn in Manning. It took him nearly three months to paint, and when he was finished, it stretched across the better part of three walls in the 450-seat auction barn. "At first I decided to have advertisements painted on [the blank walls]," Manning Sale Barn owner Robert Dappen told the *Omaha World-Herald,* "but then I had a better idea." A great big beef mural, designed to help people appreciate how much work went into their meat.

★ ★

Who knew that steak could be so exciting?

The Sale Barn was slated for demolition in 2000, and the new owner of the building offered the mural to the Audubon Historical Society. The only problem? It was an if-you-want-it-come-and-get-it offer. After some head scratching and planning, the historical society recruited lots of volunteers and, for the mural's safety, moved not just the painted panels, but over 200 feet of the Sale Barn's walls as well. Then they carefully lined up and installed the wall sections at the Machinery Building in Nathaniel Hamlin Park. (And you thought painting your bathroom was a project.) Maybe that's why the society sounds so sincere in the acknowledgements section of their Cam Ross Mural flyer: "The assistance of Southside Welding and the use of two cranes is deeply appreciated."

Nathaniel Hamlin Park is located on US 71 1 mile south of downtown Audubon. Museum buildings are open May through September from 1:00 to 4:00 p.m. or by appointment. Call (712) 563-3984 for more information.

Technically Speaking, Spiders Aren't Insects

Avoca

Usually, we're not big fans of flying cars. It's a little too seen-it-done-everywhere for our tastes. Go traveling through America, and you'll soon have your fill of local garages and auto-body shops hoisting junkyard-quality cars or trucks skyward to impress passersby. Well, all you lifters of passenger vehicles 10 to 20 feet into the air, we just thought we should tell you: We are *not* impressed.

Unless, that is, you should happen to weld eight legs onto it, paint it black, and thereby turn your flying car into a giant spider. That's just what Travis and Angela Campbell did in the yard beside their dad Darwin's place, and the results are pretty impressive. The old Volkswagen Beetle makes for a perfect spider body, and those long legs, jointed in three places, hold the Beetle a good 7 to 10 feet in the air,

Check out the legs on that Volkswagen!

★ ★

depending on where you take your measure. Stand beside the sculpture and you'll have a bug's trapped-in-the-web view of a spider: It's an arachnophobe's nightmare come true.

According to Darwin, the yard might have been even more impressive (or frightening) if he hadn't put his foot down. "They did the spider, and then they wanted me to get them a Cadillac so they could make a grasshopper. But I said, 'Nope, we stop at the spider.'" Kids . . . They don't know how to stop at just one giant automobile creature.

Besides being just a really cool piece of art, the spider showcases the family's welding talents—Darwin is the owner of Campbell's Welding and Repair. If we needed eight very long legs welded onto a car, we know exactly where we'd take our business.

The only problem with the sculpture, so far as we can tell, is the collision of two different classes of creatures: You see, contrary to popular misconception, spiders aren't insects. Beetles are, of course. But a beetle posing as an arachnid is only a problem if you're a stickler for details.

The Spider Beetle is located in downtown Avoca at the corner of West Washington and South Chestnut Streets.

Caution: Tree Growing Ahead
Brayton

We drivers of Iowa's thousands of miles of unpaved roads are used to watching for country hazards: combines and tractors, deer and cattle, and, surely the most unpredictable of the lot, bored rural youths out riding their four-wheelers all over the county. But who but the most cautious of drivers keeps an eye out for crossing trees?

That's just what you should do, though, if you find yourself southeast of Brayton on a Sunday drive. At the intersection of 350th and Nighthawk, there's a magnificent tree in the middle of the road, six stories tall with a trunk you and a friend probably can't stretch your arms around to hold hands (unless your friend's in the NBA).

Caution: Tree crossing.

Technically, the tree isn't crossing the road but just sitting there, or growing there, as it's been doing since the mid-nineteenth century, we would guess, before there were any roads around here to get in the middle of. And while we're no tree experts, it looks like a mighty

★ ★

oak. Or maybe an elm. (Hey, we told you we're no experts.) Someone's slapped a couple of patches of brightly colored paint on its
trunk, a tree's version of a jogger's reflective vest, and there's a stop
sign facing each way to remind you of the terribly obvious no matter which of the four directions you approach the tree from—north,
south, east, or west.

It doesn't look as if anyone's ever had a run-in with this tree so
reminiscent of Iowa's politics, neither too left nor too right, but right
smack dab in the center. Of course, you certainly don't want to be
the first to greet it with your grill. So keep your eyes on the road,
your hands firmly on the wheel, and remember to always, always
brake for road trees.

The tree in the middle of the road is located in Brayton, just north
of I-80 a few miles west of exit 70. Take exit 70 and head north to
350th Street, then take a left on 350th and travel about 4 miles to
the tree in the road. If you don't have a four-wheel-drive vehicle, you
should consider continuing past the turn for 350th and taking a left
on 340th Street west instead. Travel 4 miles to Nighthawk Avenue,
take a left, and then go 1 mile south to the tree in the road.

So Where Are All the Squirrels?
Council Bluffs

Built in 1885, Council Bluffs' Squirrel Cage Jail, a three-story rotating
cell drum inside a cage with only one opening per floor, was hailed
as an improvement over other jails of the period. And that thought
will make you even more terrified if you choose to visit.

Here's a more detailed description of how it works. The central
drum is composed of three floors of circular cellblocks (or cell cir-
cles?), each divided into ten pie-shaped cells. When the jailer wished
to gain access to one of the prisoners, he merely rotated the drum so
that the cell door lined up with the opening. All the prisoners took a
ride round the circle, then, so that one could be let out. (At least they
got a change of direction, if not of scenery, once in a while.)

Of course, all that squirrel-cage convenience came with a price tag. The total cost of the building was about $30,000, but only $8,000 of it went to the exterior structure. The rest covered the cost of the rotary unit—the drum, the cage, and the massive gears—that spun the prisoners, lazy-Susan style, at least a couple of times a day.

William H. Brown and Benjamin F. Bough, the inventors of the contraption, said their goal was to provide "maximum security with minimum jailer attention." But in the end, it was the minimum inmate safety that forced Council Bluffs to close the jail because in the event of a fire or other emergency, only three men at a time could be released from their cells.

The Squirrel Cage Jail is located downtown in Council Bluffs at 226 Pearl Street, right next to the railroad museum. Call (712) 323-2509 for more information.

We Grow Everything Big in Iowa

Dunlap

We grow our kids big here in Iowa. If you have any doubt about that, just go to a high school football game some Friday night in the fall and check out the size of the linemen. Big. Thick-necked. Like someone's been fertilizing them along with the corn.

So maybe you won't be surprised if you're driving north on US 30 just south of Dunlap and see a really big girl way up ahead on the side of the road. Not "big" as in heavy. Just really big—you know, Iowa big.

But as you get closer and the girl looms ever larger, you'll realize: "Okay, this girl's an honest-to-goodness freak of nature." Not really, though. She's a work of art, a wonderful example of something the girl's creator calls "giant cutout paintings." About 16 feet tall and made out of multiple sheets of painted plywood joined together, the girl's dressed in saddle shoes, baggy blue jeans, and a blue-and-white-striped shirt. Her long brown hair is in pigtails, and she's lifting a torn teddy bear and looking down at an 8-foot-tall Dalmatian with

★ ★

Big girl isn't a euphemism here.

a sour expression on her face that some people think is mad and others say is sad. (I personally think it's sad-mad.)

John Cerney, a muralist from Salinas, California, created the work, called *Little Girl Crying* (thus giving support to the sad-face theorists), and in 1999 installed it close to the east edge of US 30 on the Hein family farm. "I'm old friends with Mr. and Mrs. Hein's son, Richard," he told me, "and they agreed to let me put something up on their property." I wondered whether the Heins knew beforehand that that "something" would be an ambiguously emotional 16-foot-tall girl.

Actually, *Little Girl Crying* is a replacement for an earlier giant cut-out painting John put up in the very same spot in 1997. Titled *Iowa Landscape,* it featured the same Dalmatian flanked on the left by a 15-foot-tall wife, dressed in khaki shorts and a white button-down oxford, and on the right by a 16-foot-tall husband (exactly where the girl now stands), dressed in a smart all-blue weekend-chores ensemble. The giant husband was holding a painting of an Iowa farm scene up to the Heins' Iowa farm, a hammer in one hand, and the giant wife was holding her arm straight out in the air with her head cocked a bit to the side, as if helping him position it just right before hanging it. It's wonderful—I've seen pictures. And apparently Mr. Hein liked it, too. "I think he liked it, and liked people knowing that he was the one who let someone put up something so unusual on his land," John said. "He would even go out and clean it."

It went to a more appropriate home (in front of a frame shop in California), but John kept the Dalmatian, dreamt up (and then painted) the little girl scolding him, and then attached giant girl to giant husband's old post. He didn't get paid for the work, and that's the case with a number of his cutout paintings: John simply creates a giant work in his studio (he uses live models—normal sized, of course) and then tries to find someone with land along a busy road out in the country to let him put it up.

"I love that moment when you're driving along a road and you see something and you say, 'What is *that*? Why is that there?'" John says. Funny he should like that feeling, because he's inspired it in a whole lot of Iowans.

You'll find *Little Girl Crying* about 3 miles south of Dunlap on US 30. She's facing south, so it's best to approach from the south. John's also installed a giant cutout painting on IA 141 in Granger. Titled *Treasure Hunt,* it features two kids (giant, of course) who've dug up a treasure chest full of old toys, including that old favorite, the Etch-A-Sketch. You can find photographs of his work at www .johncerney.com.

Mill Your Flour the Danish Way

Elk Horn

The area around Elk Horn and Kimballton was settled by Danish immigrants, and a fair majority of the people who live here now are their descendants, which makes present-day Elk Horn the largest rural Danish settlement in the United States.

★ ★

Your number one source for Danish flour in the Midwest.

A lot of people have miniature windmills in their gardens, but one Elk Horn Dane, Harvey Sornson, was a bit more ambitious. When he learned that many Danish windmills were at risk of being lost to decay and neglect, he decided to try to raise enough money to dismantle a windmill in Denmark, ship it to Iowa, and then rebuild it in Elk Horn. What was first called a "crazy idea" became a rallying point for the town. Within days townspeople had raised $30,000, and the project was under way.

The Danish carpenter who dismantled the windmill came up with an ingenious way of aiding the Elk Horners in their rebuilding project: He numbered each beam from the windmill; created a perfect 6-foot-tall replica, with correspondingly numbered beams, of course; and shipped both the dismantled mill and the model to America. "All we had to do was put the pieces of the puzzle back into the right spots," one volunteer is reported to have said.

The windmill is now the only authentic operating Danish windmill in America, and it'll probably remain the one and only. Denmark passed a law shortly after the Elk Horn windmill emigrated to America declaring it illegal to ship windmills out of the country. The mill is an official Iowa Welcome Center, and visitors can climb to the top of it, see the 2,000-pound grinding stones, and watch the blades turn on a windy day. And if the Dutch flour ground at Pella's famous windmill doesn't suit your fancy, you can get your Danish flour here.

Take I-80, exit 54, and head 6 miles north. Elk Horn is at the intersection of IA 173 and CR F58. The windmill is right in the center of town, and you really can't miss it. Trust us. For more information, call (712) 764-7472.

A Long-Abandoned Farm Implement
Exira

Picture, if you will, this legend: It starts with an Iowa farmer plowing his field in the early 1860s. No one knows this farmer's name, by the way, so let's call him Chet. So Chet's going about his business, using mules hooked up to a steel plow, when a bunch of Union soldiers come marching by. Remember, this is the early 1860s, so the Civil War is in full swing. Reportedly, these soldiers were on their way to battle, and being that there were no Civil War battles fought on

★ ★

Iowa soil, they had a lot of marching ahead of them. Chet sees these soldiers, and he is inspired. Either inspired or really tired of plowing. Either way, Chet unhitches his mules, rests his plow against a teeny burr-oak sapling, and steps in line with the soldiers. He never returns.

This is the story, anyway, and it leaves one with many questions. Wasn't Chet's family worried sick about him? I mean, here he is out plowing, and then he just disappears into thin air. Maybe he wrote once he got to wherever it was the soldiers were going. He must have; otherwise, how would we now know the specifics behind his disappearance? Or was there a nosy neighbor who saw the whole thing? Did Chet grow to regret his choice, or was he totally confident in abandoning his farm and plowing duties? And who took over

The lesson here? Don't leave good farm implements near trees for longer than a decade or two. Clint Buckner

★ ★

those duties? He'd obviously made no arrangements since this was such a spur-of-the-moment deal. And what about the mules? Did they know their way back to the barn?

"How about the plow?" you ask. "What happened to Chet's trusty plow?" That, I'm happy to report, is about all we do know about Chet's situation. Nothing happened to his plow. It's still there, and the teeny oak has grown mightily around it. All that's visible is a bit of the blade sticking out of one side and a bit of the handle sticking out the other. And the tree is huge—nearly 100 feet tall. It sits on the edge of five-acre Plow in the Oak Park just outside of Exira. There's a picnic shelter nearby as well as a grill and restroom facilities. The park is surrounded by cornfields, cornfields that could have been Chet's had he stuck around.

To get to Plow in the Oak Park from Des Moines, take I-80 west to US 71 north. You'll see it on the left side before you hit Exira.

A Naval Town amid Oceans of Farmland
Farragut

The town is named for a naval hero, the main street is named for his flagship vessel, the high school nickname is the Admirals, and local businesses play on the theme with blue-and-white paint jobs and names like the Hair Dock. But besides the Nishnabotna River, which winds just outside of town, there isn't a large body of water near this tiny agricultural town.

"There are anchors all over the place, and there isn't water anywhere," local farmer and poet Michael Carey good-humoredly points out. "Plus, you're going about 60 and come into town and slow down to 25 at the sign that says DAMN THE TORPEDOES! FULL STEAM AHEAD!"

Michael's referring to Farragut's town billboard, which features the most famous quote from its namesake's illustrious naval career. Farragut was the navy's first admiral and a Civil War hero, most notably for his successful capture of Mobile Bay, the Confederate's last significant port city. During this capture Admiral Farragut lashed himself to

"But officer, the sign told me to drive like this." Berit Thorkelson

his mainsail to see over the mine (aka torpedo) smoke and called out, "Damn the torpedoes! Go ahead. Four bells!" (The quote has since been translated out of Navalese for poetic effect.)

The town's first name, in 1870, was actually Lowland, then Lawrence, but the area's first few settlers still weren't happy. One of those settlers was Major U. D. Coy, who had fought in the Black Hawk and Mexican Wars. (He also enlisted in the Civil War with his eldest son but was sent home because of his age.) Though other residents suggested Coyville, Major Coy demurred, suggesting they instead go with Farragut, a man U. D. admired. The others agreed, and in 1872 the name became official.

Every single street in town is named in connection to Admiral Farragut. Union-supporting politicians Clay and Webster each have a street, as do Civil War naval heroes Worden and Foote. Others are named after crucial Confederate forts that the admiral captured, his ships, and the president who started the American navy (Washington). Even the newest street in town, Cushing, is named for a Civil War commander whom Farragut admired. Apparently even recent-day residents agree with the founders' sentiments: Damn the lack of water. A naval theme it is!

Farragut is located in the southwestern corner of Iowa, south of IA 2 between US 275 and US 59.

A Patriotic Painter and His Rock

Greenfield

"It's a rock in the middle of nowhere, and someone paints it every Memorial Day to honor veterans," the man told me. Of course, I had asked him about curiosities. It's a frequent topic of conversation for me. "I think his name is Bubba," he said. I pictured a big farmer in overalls, seed cap on his head, probably did two tours of duty in Vietnam.

Boy, was I wrong. Ray "Bubba" Sorensen isn't a vet, he doesn't seem to favor overalls, and he was just a skinny nineteen-year-old art

★ ★

This patriotic rock really gets spruced up to celebrate Memorial Day.

student when he first decided to paint a roadside rock in Greenfield. It was 1999, and Bubba had just seen the movie *Saving Private Ryan.* With a deepened appreciation for the great sacrifices our military men and women make for us, Bubba painted a patriotic scene on a local boulder, for years covered in graffiti, as a way of saying thank-you. "I had to talk my mom into buying me some paint," he told me, "since I was just a poor college student." That first painting was a

★ ★

re-creation of the famous World War II picture of a group of American soldiers raising the flag on Iwo Jima and the words "Thank you Veterans for our freedom." It was really good, and veterans loved it.

His work got painted over a few months later, so the next year vets encouraged Bubba to paint the rock again. After he did, people stopped painting graffiti on the rock entirely. The rest is history: Bubba's painted the rock every year since, and it's come to be known as Freedom Rock.

One of my favorite paintings is from 2005. On the largest side of the rock, two men, one old and one young, embrace. On the left is Pearl Harbor survivor Houston James, and on the right Marine Staff Sergeant Mark Graunk Jr., who, the boulder tells us, lost a hand, leg, and eye while defusing a bomb in Iraq. His prosthetic arm is clearly visible. Just thinking about the image now makes me tear up.

While Bubba was painting the rock in 2006, some veterans stopped and asked if they could spread the ashes of friends at the site. "It was really windy that day—you know how windy it can get here in Iowa," Bubba told me. "I was worried about the ashes just blowing away. So I told them I could mix the ashes right into the paint." The men loved the idea, and the rock now contains the ashes of fifteen different vets. "It's become a kind of memorial," Bubba said.

When we spoke he was hard at work on his 2009 Freedom Rock painting—we'd had lots of spring rain, so he was a little behind schedule. There are a lot of Iowans (count me among them) who can't wait to see how he's going to use his great talent to honor our veterans next.

To find the Freedom Rock, travel I-80 37 miles west of Des Moines and take exit 86. Go 1 mile south on IA 25 and the rock will be on your left. Together Bubba and his wife Maria run Sorensen Studios, where they specialize in portrait photography, painting, and graphic design. Find them at www.sorensenstudios.us.

★ ★

Dirt of a Different Color in Rodeotown
Sidney

Somehow it makes sense that a collection of dirt from around the world would find a home in Rodeotown USA. After all, dirt is a big part of rodeos, maybe even third on the list of importance, right after the horses and the cowpokes. And who knew that Rodeotown USA was right here in Iowa? One might guess it to be in Texas, or Montana, possibly even one of the Dakotas. But here it is in Sidney, said to have one of the biggest rodeos in the country, nestled into the rolling pastoral farmland of southwestern Iowa.

Buildings in downtown Sidney play off its Western moniker with weathered-wood siding and beams. One such facade gives way to the Fremont County Historical Museum, a former mechanic's garage

There's lots of dirt on them there shelves! Berit Thorkelson

that now preserves the past. The dirt is in the museum's back room, right by the old garage door. There are two racks: one for American dirt and another for imported dirt. The 159 specimens are kept in tiny glass jars, once used for sampling cream, affixed with typed labels proclaiming the dirt's origin. All were gathered by or gifted to Uva Turnbull, a Freemont County resident who passed away in 1970.

"When the museum first wanted to accept the donation, I thought they were crazy," said Evelyn Birkby, a local author, columnist, and museum tour guide. But Evelyn changed her tune once she saw how much visitors loved the stuff. They're encouraged to hold the glass jars for up-close views of the dirt: the fine, sparkling black sand from Hawaii; the dusty, light-brown powder from North Africa; the coarse, saltlike grains from Florida; the chunky, orange-red clumps from Korea.

A sheet of paper by the exhibit states that the dirt "shows that no matter where a person might live, even simple cream jars and scoops of soil can transport a person into far places and into a deeper appreciation of the lands and history of our world." It may also show that 159 bottles of just about anything can be kinda cool to look at.

The Fremont County Historical Museum is located in downtown Sidney (intersection of IA 2 and US 275) at 801 Indiana Avenue on the east side of Courthouse Square. It's open from 1:00 to 4:00 p.m. on summer Sundays, with special hours over Memorial Day weekend and Rodeo Week, and by appointment. Call (712) 374-2335 or (712) 374-2320.

Where White Is a Way of Life
Stanton

Nearly all the houses in Stanton are white. A few renegades have stretched the theme and gone for a pale shade of yellow or even beige, and when it comes to shutters and trim, it's true that anything goes, but that's about as crazy as it gets.

★ ★

"I'd say it's about 90 percent white," says Don Hicks, a local schoolteacher and coach who paints houses in town during summer breaks. "I don't know that there was ever an ordinance or anything, and I've never heard of any pressure. Most everybody has just followed the tradition without being forced to."

It's unclear how that tradition started. A document at the town's Swedish Heritage and Cultural Center explains that "long ago . . . townspeople announced plans to paint every house in Stanton white." Even the Burlington Railroad got on board and painted their Stanton station white instead of the traditional red. Travelers who saw the town from the train nicknamed it the "Little White City."

Stanton still proudly proclaims this moniker on its town billboard. Go ahead and make jokes—it's not like anyone's expecting a tiny town in southwestern Iowa to be a beacon of multiculturalism, especially given its roots. The town was founded by a Swedish minister who offered plots only to nondrinking, nongambling, God-fearing Swedes. Today's phone book still features a healthy number of Johnsons, Petersons, Nelsons, and Olsons.

This last name conjures Stanton's celebrity, Virginia Christine, also known as Mrs. Olson of Folger's Coffee fame. The town celebrates Virginia in its two water towers—one's a coffeepot, the other a coffee cup. Both feature rosemaling and are, of course, white.

Mrs. Olson and the art of rosemaling are Scandinavian and therefore fit nicely with the town's roots. People tend to pin the white-house thing to these roots as well, which is ironic considering traditional Swedish houses are actually the color of the Burlington Railroad's traditional stations—red.

To get to the Little White City from Des Moines, take I-80 west to US 71. Go south on US 71 to US 34, then head west into Stanton.

Bed-and-No-Breakfast—at Your Own Risk
Villisca

It's the site of Iowa's worst mass murder, even though it happened back in 1912. Much of the draw is the unknown, as the murders remain unsolved. What is known: On a Sunday evening in June, someone entered the J. B. Moore home in tiny Villisca and murdered J. B., his wife, and four kids, plus two young girls who were spending the night. All the bodies were arranged neatly in their beds and covered with sheets. All the shades were drawn, and fabric hung over the doors and mirrors. The murder weapon, an axe, rested neatly inside the downstairs guest bedroom.

Darwin and Martha Linn bought the house in 1994 and proceeded to restore it to the way it was at the time of the murders, furniture

See you in the morning—we hope! Berit Thorkelson

★ ★

placement and all. The couple leads home tours during which they impart tons of creepy murder details and the many different (and sordid) theories as to the killer's identity. They'll top off the tour in the cemetery, if you're so inclined.

Since the tours began, there have also been paranormal investigators, documentarians, and a good number of tourists. A good enough number, in fact, that the Linns added special lamp-lit tours and overnight stays. That's right—you can spend the night where eight people were murdered. (Don't forget that they didn't have indoor plumbing in 1912.) Some overnighters, even disbelievers, have left the house seriously shaken up, and not just because they realized how crazy it was that they decided to stay over in the first place. They say they feel things. And see things. Really.

It's worth noting that the Linns have never spent the night in the Axe Murder House. "I've never had any desire to," Darwin says, "and to be honest with you, I'm sure there's something there, and until I know what it is, I'm not staying overnight. So maybe I never will."

To get to Villisca from Des Moines, take I-80 west to US 71 south. Daytime tours of the Axe Murder House start at the Olson-Linn Museum at 323 East Fourth Street, off the town square in downtown Villisca. Admission is charged. Hours are 9:00 a.m. to 4:00 p.m. on weekdays and 1:00 to 4:00 p.m. on weekends. For more information, or for rates or scheduling lamp-lit tours and overnight stays, call (712) 621-4291 or visit www.villiscaiowa.com.

5

Northwest

The Northwest is *where the wind blows in Iowa. It blows in other places, too, just not quite as strong. Almost on its own, the Northwest places us third in wind-energy production, just behind Texas and California.*

You can take a self-guided tour of a wind farm outside Storm Lake to get up close and personal, or, in Orange City, you can step into a phone booth in the shape of a windmill. It looks as though the phone's windmill-powered. It's not. But then again, it might be, depending on where Orange City gets its power.

The granddaddy of all Iowa curiosities is here in the Northwest: West Bend's Grotto of the Redemption. If you see only one curiosity in Iowa, it should probably be this man-made mountain of semiprecious gems and stones. It's either a hobby gone horribly wrong or a work of devotional genius.

There's a mountain up in Sac City, too, this one made of popcorn, sitting in its own little red shed on Main Street. It's not officially the World's Largest Popcorn Ball just yet because they made it only a few weeks ago, but it will be. And as long as we're on the big theme, there's a giant statue of Pocahontas in Pocahontas, a 168-foot-tall modernist bell tower on Jefferson's town square, and a 33-foot-tall stainless-steel statue of Jesus in Sioux City.

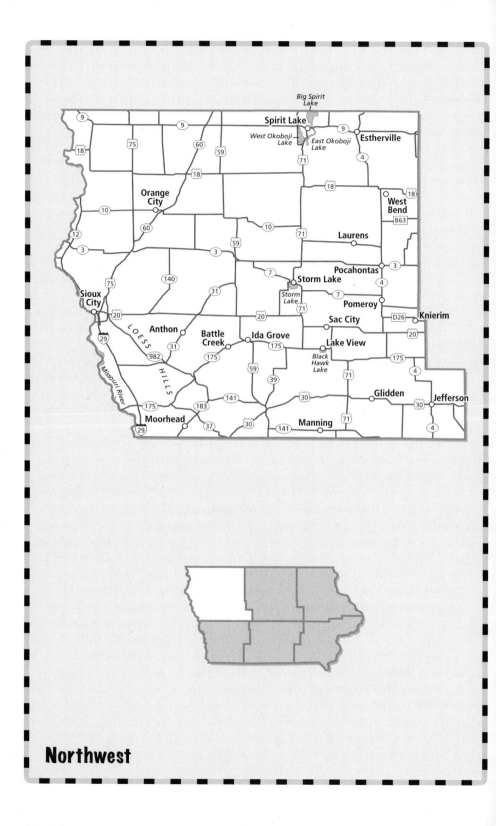

★ ★

Museum Full of Neat Junk

Battle Creek

What happens when an Iowa kid who likes to root around in field and stream grows older, but not necessarily up, and can no longer fit his collection of fossils, rocks, and bones into his garage? He assembles a like-minded board of directors with names like Big R and Bomb. He gets state and local permits enabling him to gather roadkill. He calls zoos and tells them he's interested in any upcoming dead animals. He finds himself a good taxidermist, gets himself a building, and puts all his acquisitions inside and calls it a museum, in this case, Battle Hill Museum of Natural History in Battle Creek.

"My theory is that John Q. Public and family don't sit around the breakfast table and say, 'Let's go to a museum and learn something,'" says founder and curator Dennis Laughlin, who drives a four-wheeler with a simulated reptile-skin paint job to the museum to let guests in by appointment. "You go to see a lot of neat junk, and if you learn something in the process, great."

This is not to imply that the museum houses just a bunch of junk. Dennis has acquired quite an assemblage of interesting stuff since opening the museum doors in 1990, so much so that he's added two more buildings, turned the garage into a showroom, and even turned the basement into a cave. ("All it is is some chicken wire, newspaper, aluminum, two-by-fours, and cardboard.") The place is stuffed with rocks, geodes, fossils, artifacts, antlers, an eagle, a black bear, ancient bison skulls, a two-headed calf, a 12,000-pound African elephant skeleton, a snow leopard, a Bengal tiger, and more—much, much more.

There's a moose in the museum that gets a lot of attention, since Iowans were calling in sightings of the great animal to news stations back in 1989 until a poacher shot the thing. Parts of the moose were reportedly fed to people at a local shelter before its head found a home, amid much controversy, at Battle Hill Museum.

But Dennis calls the African elephant, which died in a zoo, his "grand prize." He has photos of the entire taxidermy process, from

★ ★

A museum for the kid in you. Clint Buckner

skinning to dipping parts in a peroxide-filled kiddie pool in his back-yard to skeletal assembly.

"I get to build rocks, and I'd never gotten to skin an elephant before. I just like to do this," Dennis says. But it's not all about the kid in him, it's about actual kids, as school groups regularly tour the museum. "If there's a kid who likes dinosaurs, I guarantee he'll go home with a dinosaur bone," Dennis says. "When you get a kid in here that's genuinely interested, that's as good as it gets."

The Battle Hill Museum of Natural History is on IA 175 on the northeast side of Battle Creek. It's open by appointment; call (712) 365-4414.

The Man Who Hiccuped for Sixty-nine Years

Ask ten different people how to cure hiccups, and you're likely to get ten different answers. It seems every armchair expert has his or her method of choice. Some swear by breathing into a paper bag for ten seconds; others claim holding your breath and swallowing when you feel a hiccup coming on does the trick; and a few daring, more acrobatic folk recommend taking a full glass of water, bending way forward, and drinking with head upside down, lips on the glass's far edge.

It's likely that Charles Osborne, longtime Anthon resident and lifelong hiccuper, had heard of all these hiccup cures and more. And not a single one of them worked for him. Osborne may be one of the least fortunate, semifamous Iowans in the history of the state, since he went down in the *Guinness Book of World Records* for hiccuping every one and a half seconds on average, from 1922 until his death in 1991. (If you want a little context, Charles hiccuped almost as often as his heart beat and about three times more frequently than he took breaths.) That's a total of more than 430 million hiccups over sixty-nine years. And Osborne hiccuped longer than a lot of people live.

Anthon hasn't erected any monuments to Osborne yet, though he surely deserves one for having made it through a life of hiccuping. Perhaps his constant hiccuping in a small town where people like their peace and quiet annoyed the wrong folks—everyone? Give Anthon a few more years for its frayed nerves to heal, though, and they'll form a committee, pound the pavement for donations, have a bake sale, and commission a bronze statue of Osborne with his mouth slightly open and a grimace on his poor face.

Anthon is about 20 miles southeast of Sioux City on IA 31.

★ ★

Is This My Meteorite?
Estherville

On May 10, 1879, the largest meteorite known to have fallen in North America planted itself 14 feet deep on Sever Lee's farm about 3 miles north of Estherville. When Lee didn't show much interest in the rock, a group of young men hired a well digger, George Osborn, to help them raise it. It weighed 437 pounds. Realizing the potential value of the meteorite, the boys loaded it onto a wagon with a large sign that read, "I am the heavenly meteor. I arrived May 10th at 5 o'clock. From whence I came nobody knows, but I am enroute for Chicago." (A surprisingly well-spoken but very enigmatic meteorite.)

The group didn't get too far to Chicago before they heard rumors that their ownership was being challenged, so they returned to Estherville and first buried the meteorite in Osborn's cornfield and then transferred it to a group member's home. Meanwhile, Keokuk attorney Charles Birge had discovered that Sever Lee defaulted on his farm payments and, making successful claim to the land, obtained a writ of attachment to the meteorite and summarily took it from the boys. Later he sold it to the British Museum of Natural History in London for what was rumored to be a large sum of money. Poor Sever Lee didn't know what hit him or his former farm.

The meteorite that landed in Lee's field was only one of three large pieces that fell around Estherville that day. Witnesses saw what appeared to be a fireball traveling across the sky from the southeast to northwest, and two people 6 miles west of Estherville reported seeing the meteorite split into three pieces, with the three vapor trails making what appeared to be a crow's foot in the sky. Taking into account the other two pieces and the more than 5,000 smaller fragments that were collected by residents—"gathering meteors" became a favorite leisure activity for Estherville residents for a couple of years—experts estimated the Estherville meteorite had a total weight of around 744 pounds, making it the largest meteor to have landed in North America.

★ ★

Estherville's meteorite is now housed in museums all over the world, including the National Museum of Natural History in Paris, the Natural History Museum of Vienna, the National Museum in Washington DC, the Field Museum in Chicago (Mr. Heavenly Meteor did, in fact, make it to Chicago after all), and the Peabody Museums at Yale, Harvard, and Amherst. Estherville wouldn't have anything but small meteorite pebbles and keepsakes (residents crafted larger fragments into rings) were it not for the generosity of the University of Minnesota, which loaned the chamber of commerce a chunk of their 151-pound specimen for display in the town's beautifully renovated 1903 Carnegie Library. Estherville also placed a boulder with a bronze tablet to mark the spot where the largest piece fell on Lee's farm.

Estherville's Carnegie Library, which contains a fragment of the second meteorite chunk to be discovered, is located in downtown Estherville. For more information, call (712) 362-7731. You can also visit the boulder and bronze plaque, located 2 miles north of Estherville on IA 4, which marks the hole (or marks a spot precisely 432 feet west of the hole) where the 437-pound meteorite fell on Lee's farm.

A Son's Tribute Gone Awry
Glidden

Colonel Paul Tibbets, World War II B-29 bomber pilot, paid his mother the great tribute of naming his plane after her. What a proud moment that must have been for his mom, an Iowa native hailing from the small town of Glidden, when she learned that the plane that carried her son and his crew on their perilous journeys and brought them safely home again, mission after mission, was named in her honor. And then came Little Boy.

On August 6, 1945, Colonel Tibbets and his crew dropped the first atomic bomb, "Little Boy," on Nagasaki. The name of the plane that delivered the bomb, of course, was the *Enola Gay*.

The Tibbets have moved away from Glidden, but the legacy of *Enola Gay* and Colonel Paul Tibbets lives on in Glidden, albeit in a humble form. The family donated a picture of the *Enola Gay,* which now hangs in the public library.

Glidden is on US 30, east of Carroll. The Glidden Public Library is located downtown, at 131 Idaho Street. Call (712) 659-3781 for more information.

Small Iowa Town, Big Medieval Style
Ida Grove

Byron Godbersen had a thing for castles. Being a millionaire, he also had the means to indulge in his fascination. We're not talking about a scale-models-in-the-basement type of indulgence, here; we're talking about full-on castles built around Byron's hometown of Ida Grove.

Entering the town from the west is a surreal experience. There's the huge stone observation tower/city marker, the stone-towered suspension bridge on the local golf course, and all the castle-themed buildings connected with Midwest Industries, the manufacturing company Byron founded and one of the city's top employers. For example, armored knights stand watch at the stone gate in front of the Midwest Industries facility designed to test and display products like boat hoists. From the gate you can see eight-acre Lake LaJune, named for Byron's wife, which was once an eight-acre cornfield. On it floats a half-scale replica of the HMS *Bounty,* a late eighteenth-century full-rigged merchant ship.

And that's not all. Byron thought the town of about 2,300 needed a second newspaper, so he started the *Ida County Courier* and designed that downtown building like a castle, too. He also built the aptly named Skate Palace, with its flag-topped turrets and wood-heavy medieval interior. Other local non-Byron businesses, like Kastle Kones, play off the established theme.

Byron was one of few people whose home was literally his castle, a far cry from the farmhouse in which he grew up. (He passed away in May of 2003, but LaJune still lives there.) Byron's attempt to make

A newspaper housed in royal digs. Clint Buckner

farm life easier led to his fortune. Midwest Industries' first product was a hydraulic hoist for farm wagons, and things only grew from there. Byron remains Iowa's most prolific inventor, with more than fifty patents to his name.

The question remains: Why castles? The best answer I could dig up was that on a trip to Europe, Byron was struck by the stone structures he saw. He returned to Iowa and, bit by bit, began to turn Ida Grove into a kind of medieval Iowan Mayberry, a place where castles meet Kum and Go.

From Sioux City, head east on US 20, then south on US 59 into Ida Grove. For more information, contact the Ida Grove Chamber of Commerce at (712) 364-3404 or visit www.idagrovechamber.com.

★ ★

Lighthouse on the Prairie

Jefferson

Built in the sixties, Jefferson's bell tower on the square is flagrantly modern, if you know what we mean. And though it strikes a discordant note at first glance—a 168-foot-tall modern bell tower in the middle of an Iowa farm town—the more you look at it, the more it grows on you. Think of it as a lighthouse overlooking a sea of prairie. And then, when the electronic carillon begins to play "America the Beautiful" (of course, the carillon is electronic in a 1960s bell tower), you just might fall in love.

You can take a tour, and a glass elevator ride to the top, and look out on beautiful America from the observation deck, which sits twelve stories high above the town. The carillon chimes every quarter hour, but it also plays religious and patriotic music at 11:00 a.m., 2:00 p.m., and 5:00 p.m. daily.

Jefferson is also home to a telephone museum. You can trace the evolution of the phone from the hand-crank jobbies you see in movies (with the mouthpiece on the phone box) to the more modern models you're familiar with. If you're the type who not only hates cell phones but gets shivers when you feel rotary-phone plastic wrapped tightly around your index finger, this museum will send you into ecstasies of nostalgia.

The bell tower, officially known as the Mahanay Memorial Carillon Tower, is at the corner of Lincoln Way and Wilson Street in downtown Jefferson and is open daily Memorial Day to Labor Day from 11:00 a.m. to 4:00 p.m., on weekends in May and September, and at other times by appointment (call 515-386-2155). The museum is located at 105 West Harrison Street and is open Monday through Friday, 9:00 a.m. to 5:00 p.m. For more information, call (515) 386-4141 or visit www.gojacc.com/attractions.

✫ ★

A Napoleon-Complex Couple

Knierim

At 4 feet 10 inches and 85 pounds and 5 feet 7 inches and 127 pounds, respectively, Bonnie Parker and Clyde Barrow made for a decidedly unimposing pair. Of course, looks can be deceiving. In a little more than two years, the couple killed a dozen people (including nine lawmen), kidnapped many others, and robbed countless small-town banks and businesses during the early 1930s.

Ian Frazier, in his book *Great Plains,* gives this description of Bonnie and Clyde: "Clyde had on his right arm the tattoo of a girl and the name 'Grace.' Bonnie had on the inside of her right thigh a tattoo of two hearts joined by an arrow, with 'Bonnie' in one heart and 'Roy' in the other. They kept a white rabbit, and took it with them on their travels. Clyde also brought along his saxophone and sheet music. Bonnie read *True Romance* magazines, painted her toenails pink, and dyed her hair red to match her hats, dresses, and shoes."

According to one police investigator, Bonnie and Clyde loved to drive fast and far and "thought nothing of driving a thousand miles at a stretch." On one of these junkets in 1934 (just months before they were shot dead in a police ambush near Gibsland, Louisiana), they stopped for a brief visit in Knierim (pronounced *ke-neer-em*) to make a $272 withdrawal from the bank. Of course, they didn't have an account at Knierim's bank, and they completed the transaction from behind the barrel of a gun.

Today the town of Knierim, a small group of homes beside a grain elevator, no longer has what you might think of as a downtown. The buildings are still there—hyper-plain brick structures, a couple of which have wooden false fronts that give the street a slightly Western feel—but the businesses have long since gone bust. There's a building with faded hand-painted signs that say SALOON and ICE FOR SALE, but the saloon's closed, and a trailer home has been plunked down beside it. Both Jud's Grocery and the bank Bonnie and Clyde robbed, a simple square block of a brick building, have been converted into private residences.

★ ★

Knierim is so small that when I asked a man who was helping a neighbor unload a refrigerator about the bank robbery, he said that his grandfather was waiting in line at the bank at the time of the holdup. "He said they were as friendly and polite as can be," he told me. And that means a lot to small-town Iowans—if you're going to rob, kidnap, and kill, at least do it with a smile.

Knierim is north of US 20 at the intersection of CR D26 and CR P19. The bank is right "downtown," the farthest brick building from the railroad tracks.

A Parade with Real Floats
Lake View

Here's a question: Why are parade floats called "floats"? After all, they don't really float; they roll. Granted, most so-called "float" makers deceptively cover the wheels of their creations so that they appear to float rather than roll down the street, but roll they do.

Enter Lake View and its lighted water-float parade to reestablish linguistic accuracy. Pam Wollesen, owner of Day Dreamers Gift and Souvenir Shop in downtown Lake View and thirty-six-year-veteran organizer of the town's summer water carnival, says the parade of lighted water floats "is really something else." Exactly, and that something else is a parade with honest-to-goodness floats.

The water-float parade began back in the 1950s and has since become the Black Hawk Lake Summer Water Carnival's signature event. Back then the floats were made out of cardboard on pontoons, but after rain disintegrated the floats one year, Lake View started building them out of wood. Each float is constructed on pontoons (or a pontoon boat), fitted with a generator, and then strung with lots and lots of lights. Then, when darkness falls on Sunday night, boats tow each float in a parade around the bays and inlets of Black Hawk Lake while residents and visitors watch the procession from the shore.

The town now contracts its floats out to one woman, who makes all fifteen to twenty in the parade. "People just don't have the time

★ ★

or resources to make them," Wollesen said, "so we hire out." Businesses and civic groups in town sponsor floats (or parts of floats), and residents and visitors get to sit on the shore and enjoy the parade, with floats lit up bright as Christmas trees, without ever having to smash a thumb with a hammer or step on a nail.

The Water Carnival also features a regular parade (with rolling floats), Saturday-night fireworks over the lake, a lip-sync contest, the Little Miss Black Hawk Pageant, and, miracle of miracles, a quiet tractor pull (it's a pedal-tractor pull). But the floats are the real crowd-pleasers. "It was the only water parade in the state for a long time, but now I think they might have one somewhere out east on the Mississippi. I'm not sure, though," said Wollesen. But Lake View gets credit for having the first parade in the state with floats that really float.

Lake View is located on Black Hawk Lake at the intersection of US 71 and CR M68. The Black Hawk Lake Summer Water Carnival is held the second weekend in July. For more information, call (712) 657-2664 or visit www.lakeview-ia.com/carnival.

Tower to Cessna 5RW3: We Have a Message—Fore!
Laurens

Iowa has more golfers per capita than any other state in the union, and with so much land under cultivation, we have to get a little creative about where we play. The town of Lake View, for example, hosts the Arctic Open on the first Saturday in February, with a 9-hole course on frozen Black Hawk Lake. (Participants hate the snow traps but love the fact that the only water hazard in the area is covered by 9 inches of bulletproof ice.) Then there's Des Moines' Skywalk Open, an annual 18-hole minigolf tournament held in the city's 3 miles of downtown skywalks.

But the award for the most creative and potentially dangerous alternative golf space has to go to Laurens, whose Skyways Airport is both an airport and a golf course, the Laurens Country Club. The airport

came first, and then the golfers planned a course around it, making the grass runway do double-duty as a fairway. It's one of only two golf-course airports in the country, with the other located in Wisconsin.

Golfers love the Laurens Country Club, not least of all because an airplane landing on the fairway offers a ready-made excuse for slicing into the rough. Club scorecards come printed with the reminder that airplanes, not golfers, have the runway right-of-way, and pilots don't even have to ask if they can play through. The country club does, however, ask that they circle the fairway once (and buzz the clubhouse if they feel so inclined) before landing to give golfers a chance to clear the runway.

According to course manager Carol Thomas, with a runway on the course, golfers aren't the only ones who end up in the rough. "One guy misjudged the runway and came bouncing down the rough," she said. "He ended up on the eighth green, dripping oil all over the place." She seemed so miffed by the fact that her groundskeepers had to replant the green that she didn't even say how close he came to the pin.

Laurens Skyways Airport and the Laurens Country Club are both located just west of town at 12582 Highway 10. For more information, call (712) 841-2287.

A Lawnmower Ride with Friends
Laurens

At the age of seventy-three, in poor health and with failing eyesight, Alvin Straight of Laurens rode 240 miles across Iowa to visit his ailing brother Lyle in Mount Zion, Wisconsin. On a lawnmower. His top speed was 5 miles per hour, and it took him nearly six weeks. National newspapers picked up the story, including the *New York Times,* and Hollywood called for the rights. They got them, of course.

David Lynch directed a G-rated Disney movie based on Alvin's epic journey called *The Straight Story* that was released in 1999. Most of the filming took place in Laurens and the Northeast's Clermont.

The 1966 John Deere riding lawnmower and 10-foot trailer from the movie are in Clermont, but the real tractor and trailer are in Laurens with Mrs. Darlene Chaffee.

Darlene and her husband, William (who died in early 2009), long-time co-editors of the *Laurens Sun,* were friends of Alvin's. It was they who drove out east to his brother's place in Wisconsin to bring Alvin back to Laurens, hauling his definitely worse-for-the-wear John Deere on a trailer behind their pickup. According to Mrs. Chaffee, a gentleman from Texas who heard about Alvin's trip bought him a brand-new $6,000 lawnmower as a replacement, and it wasn't long before he started making trips again on his new and improved machine. "His next trip he was going to visit family, and he got to Nebraska before he got frostbite," she told me.

And then in July of 1996, exactly two years after his original odyssey, he set out on a mower trip bound for Idaho, over 1,000 miles away. Weeks later he was found about 400 miles from Laurens near the Pine Ridge Indian Reservation in South Dakota, lying in his pull trailer, suffering from sunburn and dehydration. He was brought back to be treated at a hospital in Sioux City, but he never recovered and died there November 9, 1996. I know it's sad—but it's the straight story, too.

You can sit on either one of Alvin's tractors in Laurens. Heck, if you ask nice, Mrs. Chaffee may even let you ride one. "You can even ride it around the block if you want," she told me. "You probably wouldn't want to go any farther than that, though." I wonder if, and how often, she gave the adventurous Alvin that same advice?

She also kindly invited me to her annual 6.5-mile lawnmower ride fund-raiser in early June. That's when a group of maybe a dozen or so folks from Laurens ride mowers a few miles outside of town to a friend's farmhouse. They stop, have lemonade and cookies, and then turn around and come back. "Be sure to let me know if you're coming," she told me. "We'll want to have a lawnmower ready for you."

★ ★

You can reach Mrs. Chaffee at (712) 841-4541. Alvin's house, featured in the movie and a tourist stop for years, caught fire in the summer of 2007. Arson is suspected. It's slated for demolition, but the committee that was working to restore the home might mark the site in some way.

The Furry Barn from across the Sea
Manning

Not to be outdone by the Danish Elk Horners up the road (who shipped a windmill all the way from the Old Country to Iowa), the Manning Heritage Foundation received as a gift from Herr Claus Manning a 350-year-old authentic German Hausbarn from the village of Offenseth in Schleswig-Holstein, Germany. (In 1991, when he made the offer of the Hausbarn, Herr Claus still had tenants in the building, according to the woman at the gift shop, so Manning had to wait a few years for the people to move out.)

The thatched Hausbarn, an American adaptation from the German "farmer's house," was common to the Schleswig-Holstein region of Germany during the seventeenth and eighteenth centuries. The Hausbarn's most unusual feature? It's designed to house both the farmer's family and his livestock. Of course, such living arrangements make for cramped and decidedly aromatic conditions. And it should go without saying that if you don't wake up early, it's hell trying to get into the bathroom.

The Hausbarn was dismantled and shipped to Iowa in 1996, groundbreaking was held in 1997, and in July 1999 master carpenter Martin Hansen arrived from Germany to lead volunteers in the reconstruction. The steep thatched roof, which the gift-shop saleswomen assured me never leaked, is made from Baltic Sea reeds bunched tightly together and makes the whole building look kind of fuzzy at the eaves.

Hausbarn/Heritage Park Grove, as the site is called, also offers some beautiful grounds as well as a 1915 bungalow-style homestead that's being restored for use as a museum and exhibit. At press time

It's a house and a barn in one! Can you say "strong household odors"?

workers were also putting the finishing touches on a German-style restaurant and conference center right beside the Hausbarn, so you can get a taste of the Old Country while you network, too. And a reminder: Though the Hausbarn was originally intended for livestock as well as people, now that we have health codes and such, livestock are no longer permitted. So just leave Bessie in the trailer.

Manning is located on IA 141, 7 miles west of the intersection with US 71. The Hausbarn is just east of town on the south side of IA 141 at the intersection with Concord Road. For more information, call (712) 655-3131 or visit www.germanhausbarn.com.

★ ★

Hundreds of Miles of Hills in Iowa
Moorhead

Stretching for more than 200 miles north and south along the eastern edge of the Missouri floodplain, the Loess Hills are one of Iowa's most outstanding geological features. The hills were formed in much the same way snowdrifts or sand dunes are formed: by wind.

During the Ice Age, glaciers ground underlying rock into fine sediment called glacial flour, which was deposited on the Missouri floodplain as the glaciers melted, creating huge mudflats. When the melt waters receded, the mudflats dried, and the silt was carried by westerly winds to the east, where it was deposited over broad areas. The heavier, coarser silt deposited closest to the Missouri formed sharp, high bluffs on the western edge of the Loess Hills, whereas the

A real curiosity—hills in western Iowa.

lighter silt deposited on the Loess's eastern edge formed gently slop-
ing hills.

The end result is that western Iowa, one of the flattest regions of
the state, has a range of strikingly beautiful and geologically interesting hills and bluffs running along almost the entire length of the Missouri floodplain. Are the Loess Hills unique? Not quite, but the only
other place in the world with loess hills so tall (loess, pronounced
luss, is German for "loose" or "crumbly") is Shanxi, China.

The hills' unique geology is evident even to the untrained eye. Sharp
bluffs, irregular peaks and saddles, deep gullies, and staircase-like
features on some hillsides are all testament to the way the hills were
formed and the way they're now eroding. (The hillside staircases, called
cat steps, are actually the result of slipping soil.) Unfortunately, the
Loess Hills are incredibly fragile. Since the fine silt deposits don't contain
any clay, the material that normally binds wet soil together, the Loess
Hills have one of the highest erosion rates in the United States.

Efforts are under way to protect the Loess Hills from man-made
sources of erosion, not only to preserve the hills in their own right,
but also to hold onto one of the strongest pieces of evidence we
have to prove to out-of-staters that Iowa is most certainly not flat.

The Loess Hills stretch along almost the entire western Iowa border, with hiking, camping, and scenic drives throughout. Learn more
at the Loess Hills Hospitality Association Visitor's Center and Gift
Shop in downtown Moorhead on IA 183, open daily from 9:00 a.m.
to 4:30 p.m. in summer and 10:00 a.m. to 4:30 p.m. in winter. Call
(712) 886-5441 for additional information.

A Subtle Celebration of a Not-So-Subtle Weed
Moorhead

Sometimes it's Crabgrass Days, and other times it's more of a Crabgrass Day, or Crabgrass Afternoon, even Crabgrass Morning. And to
be honest, except for the name, there's really nothing about Moorhead's festival that has anything to do with crabgrass.

Shelia Lindsey at the Loess Hills Hospitality Association explains that when the festival in this town of about 250 started in the 1990s, people just wanted something to do in September. Because the time they chose to schedule an excuse to hang out coincided with the time of year when crabgrass is in full bloom, the community decided to name the festival for the weed. While they were at it, they declared themselves the Crabgrass Capital of Iowa.

That first year was the biggest, and there was even a contest for the largest blade of crabgrass, held in the town park. Things have calmed down significantly since that wild and crazy opener. "Now it's a relaxed day in the park for the residents of the city, an old-fashioned community get-together," Shelia says. "Some are bigger than others. There may be a potluck meal in the evening, a talent show, a dance, a cakewalk. Sometimes we have a parade. It just depends on which volunteers are active at the time and how the spirit moves them."

The year I spoke to Shelia, the festival was scheduled to consist of a community church service where residents would gather as one regardless of religious affiliation, followed by a pancake feed. When I pressed her about the absence of anything related to the festival's namesake, she said it might make a subtle appearance. "We'll have wildflowers at the church service," she told me. "We'll probably have a few sprigs of crabgrass tucked in there."

Crabgrass Days (or Day) is usually held the third weekend in September in Moorhead, located on IA 183 north of Council Bluffs. For more information, call the Loess Hills Hospitality Association at (712) 886-5441.

A Wind-Powered Phone Booth
Orange City

Okay, so the small windmill at the corner of Central Avenue and West First Street in downtown Orange City isn't really operational—the blades don't power anything, nor do they rotate a single inch, even in a good stiff prairie wind—but what the windmill lacks in authenticity it surely makes up for in originality. It may be the only pay-phone-booth windmill in the country, maybe even the world.

Orange City is yet another small Iowa town with a strong Dutch heritage, and they've got the big windmill to prove it. You can find it out on IA 10 just east of town, a 75-foot-tall, fourteen-ton windmill housing the chamber of commerce and visitor center. Orange City's downtown businesses also feature false decorative fronts painted in cheery colors to give the place a pseudo-Dutch feel, the streets are lined with tulips in spring and marigolds in summer, and the high school marching band is reported to perform in Dutch wooden shoes on special occasions (sounds downright painful).

But the most original expression of Dutch heritage in town is the windmill phone booth. Sure, phone booths have become passé and a bit neglected with the invention and meteoric rise of the cell phone, but Orange City may have found a way to keep humble pay phones alive. Turn them into Dutch windmills, and people may dig in their pockets for loose change to call home just for the sheer novelty of it all.

Orange City's windmill phone booth is located downtown, at the corner of Central Avenue and West First Street. For more information about events in Orange City, call the chamber of commerce at (712) 707-4510.

A Big American Indian Welcome
Pocahontas

The 25-foot-tall statue of Pocahontas on the outskirts of the city of Pocahontas in the county of Pocahontas certainly commands attention.

No matter what you think of her appearance, you must admit she serves her purpose. Senator Albert Shaw and his son, Frank, saw giant statues of fish and Paul Bunyan in Minnesota and thought Pocahontas, too, should have such a community symbol. What better symbol for the community of Pocahontas than its namesake

This Indian princess would dominate in the WNBA. Clint Buckner

Pocahontas? (For those of you who don't recall your elementary-school history classes, Pocahontas was the American Indian princess credited for saving the life of Captain John Smith, the English leader of the Jamestown, Virginia colonists back in the early seventeenth century.)

In 1953 Frank hired the man behind the giant muskie statue in Minnesota to design Miss Pocahontas. He then contracted his friend and fellow Poky (as town residents call themselves) Marcell Moritz to build her. During his spare time over the course of two years, Marcell crafted Pocahontas out of wood, steel, and cement. He finished in 1956. She has stood ever since, on IA 3 just east of the city, serving as a landmark and greeting visitors headed into town or on their way to or from nearby vacation destinations.

Whether for reasons of beauty or gender ambiguity, the statue is nothing if not memorable. "When you're a kid growing up, you think it's pretty cool. Then you get older and realize it's just not that attractive," said one former Pocahontas resident who wishes to remain nameless. "But it is a great conversation starter, something the town is easily recognized for. You go somewhere and people say, 'Oh, Pocahontas, I've been there. That town with the Indian.'"

A Long, Strange Trip

Pomeroy

The dancing bears on the sign outside Byron's are like Deadhead code. To the casual observer, they are, at best, a questionably cutesy choice for a place where people go to knock 'em back. To a Grateful Dead fan, they are a total trip in tiny Pomeroy, a guarantee that someone nearby is ready to listen to your stories about killer bootlegs and the Jerry Days.

The place first stands out from Pomeroy's one-block downtown because it's occupied—even the town hall has moved to the local minimall. I ran across it on a random Sunday, when owner Byron Stuart was getting ready for business. Nearly every square inch of the

A place for the tie-dye and dreads set. Clint Buckner

place was packed with Dead memorabilia, from posters and T-shirts to stuffed bears and stickers. Byron was wearing a tie-dyed T-shirt and had Dead tunes playing in the background. He told me that the motif, made up of gifts and items from his personal collection, was an accident. "It was just a generic bar, and I wasn't going to turn it into a Grateful Dead bar, but on the first day some girls brought in a framed T-shirt of Jerry Garcia, and it set the mood," he says.

Truth be told, Byron was a Deadhead long before the gift. He first saw the Dead in Des Moines in 1972, and he was hooked. The other

781 residents of Pomeroy don't necessarily share Byron's taste in music. "When I moved back here, nobody had heard of the Grateful Dead," Byron says. "Now they know the name, but maybe think it's a devil-worshiper band."

Local regulars may or may not stick around on live-music nights to hear the hippie jam bands, acoustic folk rockers, and old-school biggies Byron books from both the surrounding regions and around the country. (Canned Heat once made the trek and loved it—said it was like playing in Byron's living room.) Byron relies heavily on word of mouth as a promotional tool. Sometimes this packs 'em in, mostly from a 40-mile radius; other times it doesn't. Either way, he gets his live-music fix without having to drive for hours to a bigger city.

And then Byron's goes back to being your average small-town bar that happens to be drenched in Grateful Dead memorabilia. Byron has kindly stocked the jukebox with a wide range of music for his solid base of regulars. Every once in a while a Dead tune comes on, and when Byron catches a local compulsively tappin' his toes, he smiles.

Byron's is located at 112 Main Street. For more information, call (712) 468-2372 or visit www.downtownpomeroy.com/byron's/index .htm.

Popcorn Ball for 6,000?
Sac City

Sac City, the self-proclaimed "Popcorn Capital of the World," wouldn't think of giving up its claim to the World's Largest Popcorn Ball without a fight. And after being bested by first the Iowa Boy Scouts and then some folks from Lake Forest, Illinois, Sac City is back on top with a 7½-foot-tall, 5,060-pound behemoth. They're just waiting on official verification from Guinness, but really, for the Lake Forest gang, it's all over but the crying. Eat that, Illinois!

Sac City and the popcorn factory in town, Noble Popcorn, built their first giant popcorn ball back in 1995. After two years of giant popcorn ball visitors, they got tired of taking people to the

★ ★

warehouse where it was stored, so they stuck seven sticks of dynamite in it and blew it up in front of a crowd at the Sac County Fair.
They were expecting a shower of sugar-coated popcorn, and some

Yes it's big, but is it fresh?

★ ★

people in the grandstands even covered themselves with ponchos. Isn't it great when you need personal protective equipment at the county fair? No need really. The 2,225-pounder just split into a few big pieces, and spectators rushed the field to get a chunk of history.

In 2004 Sac Citians built another world-champion ball in celebration of the town's 150th anniversary, a 3,100-pounder that they had the wisdom to give its own giant popcorn ball display shed on Main Street so they wouldn't have to stop work every time someone from out of town wanted to see it. "It's impressive," the owner of the hotel in Sac City told me. "But it's a real popcorn ball. If you look close in the summer, you can see bugs crawling all over it." Yummy.

After the Lake Forest bunch built a 3,423-pounder to wrest Sac City's now twice-won title away, the Iowa crew went back to the drawing board and plotted to build a popcorn ball that would never be beat. In late February of 2009, a whole slew of volunteers and some folks at Noble Popcorn donned rubber gloves and packed handful upon handful of sugar- and syrup-coated popcorn to make for the third time the World's Largest Popcorn Ball. And how did they feel about it? "To us, it doesn't mean a darn thing," Noble factory owner Milo Lines told the *Des Moines Register*. "But to a tourist, it draws them in." Sac City says it will be particularly happy to show the ball to folks from Illinois.

The World's Largest Popcorn Ball has replaced the old ball in the shed on Main Street. To check out all the goodies at Noble Popcorn, go to www.noblepopcorn.com.

Monument to a Fallen Sergeant
Sioux City

In 1803 Meriwether Lewis and William Clark accepted orders from Thomas Jefferson to explore the newly acquired Louisiana Purchase and seek an all-water route to the Pacific. On May 14, 1804, the explorers headed up the Missouri; they reached the Pacific in

A memorial to a man whose luck ran out in Iowa.

★ ☆ ★ ☆ ★ ☆ ★ ☆ ★ ☆ ★ ☆ ★ ☆ ★ ☆ ★ ☆ ★ ☆ ★ ☆ ★ ☆ ★ ☆ ★ ☆ ★ ☆ ★ ☆

November 1805, and they returned to St. Louis on September 23, 1806.

Of course, quite a bit happened in between. Lewis and Clark's expedition journal entry for Monday, August 20, 1804, just three months into the journey, describes the death and burial of one Sergeant Floyd, the only member of the party to die on the two-year, four-month, nine-day, 8,000-plus-mile journey. Of all the future states in which the explorer could have bit it, he chose Iowa, and of that we can be proud.

"We buried him at the top of a high round hill," the journal reads, "overlooking the river and country for a great distance situated just below a small river without a name to which we name and call Floyd's River, the bluff Sgt. Floyd's Bluff." The round hill, the bluff, the river, and the great view are all still there, just south of Sioux City. And to honor the fallen sergeant and his great instincts about final resting places, the city built a 100-foot-tall, 717-ton white sandstone obelisk on the hill to mark his grave site. The bluff offers a panoramic view of the Missouri River and Nebraska to the west.

So how did Sergeant Floyd die? Was he killed while protecting Sacagawea from a hostile Indian raid? Was he braving rapids or scaling a cliff or wrestling a bear? Unfortunately, his death was decidedly undramatic. Modern medical authorities now believe Floyd's death was caused by complications arising from appendicitis, a condition that had no cure at the time except leeches, and those were awaiting FDA approval (hungrily, we might add).

The journal entry for the day of Floyd's death concludes, "We returned to the boat and proceeded to the mouth of little river, 30 yards wide, and camped a beautiful evening." Lewis and Clark didn't seem to lose much sleep over Sergeant Floyd's death, even on the very evening they buried him. But we all know how detached explorers can be, what with their wanderlust and fear-of-intimacy issues.

The Sergeant Floyd monument is northeast of exit 143 off I-29.

A Teetotaling Martyr

Way back in 1886, Iowa was a dry state. Not dry as in no rain—dry as in no booze. But the many bars and breweries in Sioux City managed to stay open by paying local officials what you might call a sin tax. (Bribery is another word for it.)

Minister George C. Haddock, a staunch opponent of alcohol consumption, had been preaching in favor of prohibition for years all over the Midwest, and that's how he ended up in Sioux City the night of August 3. Apparently, at least one man in town didn't buy what he was selling. Brewery foreman John Arensdorf shot Minister Haddock to death right on Fourth Street: There could have been witnesses that night, we're told, but they were probably already drunk. Arensdorf was tried and acquitted of the crime not once but twice, and legend has it that at the conclusion of the second trial, he and the jury went out for a few cold ones. There's even a picture of him on a Sioux City history Web site, allegedly out drinking with the jury.

Sioux City had either a guilty conscience or a sadistic streak when they installed a memorial to George Haddock in the exact spot where he died on the east side of Water Street, in between Third and Fourth Streets. Embedded in the asphalt is a small metal disk with a cross in the center and the words HADDOCK DIED HERE around the circumference. For more information about the murder and to see the picture of the jury, go to www.siouxcityhistory.org/people/.

Three-Story-Tall Stainless-Steel Mary and Jesus
Sioux City

Take an abandoned Catholic boarding school on a hilltop, tear it down, add a 30-foot-tall, five-ton stainless-steel statue of Mother Mary, a 33-foot-tall stainless-steel statue of Jesus, lots of landscaped gardens, and a building housing a hand-carved, life-size wooden sculpture of the Last Supper, and what do you have? Well, we're not quite sure, but it's called Trinity Heights.

Queen of Peace Inc., a nonprofit group, has spent more than $1 million erecting the towering statues and developing the fifty-three-acre site for visitors. The project began with sculptor Dale Lamhere's statue of the Immaculate Heart of Mary Queen of Peace, set in place on December 16, 1992. The statue of Jesus was erected six years later, on June 9, 1998. Made from unadorned, unpainted stainless steel, with hands and faces as gray as their robes, the sculptures appear strangely modern.

The site also contains a gift shop that sells religious books, videos, and paraphernalia, and the Saint Joseph Center Museum, which houses the life-size Last Supper carving as well as artifacts from the Trinity Schools, which once stood on the grounds. A self-taught sculptor, Jerry Traufler spent seven years carving his Last Supper with mallet and chisel. Traufler used da Vinci's painting *The Last Supper* as his model, but instead of cribbing the disciples' faces from the master, he used models from his hometown of Le Mars, including his own wife, stand-in for the disciple John, seated to the right of Christ. (There's a picture along the back wall with the Le Mars models standing over the shoulders of their respective disciple doubles.)

"Those are some big chunks of wood," my tour guide said. "Each one weighed somewhere between 200 and 300 pounds, without appendages. The hands and feet and the sandals—he made those separately so he could remove 'em. That way he could move the disciples around in his shop and not knock all the digits off their little hands." And as everyone knows, when you're working with disciples,

The Virgin Mary looking radiant.

it's important to keep all digits intact, especially when one of them happens to be your wife.

Trinity Heights, located at the corner of Thirty-third Street and Floyd Avenue, is open April through October, 9:00 a.m. to 6:00 p.m., and November through March, 10:00 a.m. to 4:00 p.m. From I-29 take the Stockyards exit (147A) to Floyd Boulevard. Travel north about 3 miles, then turn west on Thirty-third Street just after Sioux Tools. For more information, call (712) 239-8670.

World-Record House Builder
Spirit Lake

Bryan Berg, famous Iowa builder, travels all over the world doing construction projects, gets paid thousands and thousands of dollars for his services, and almost always has the delicious pleasure of knocking down his pricey buildings once they're completed. Berg's demolition tool of choice? A leaf blower.

Though it may not seem possible for a simple blower to summarily take down the equivalent of a two-story house, Berg's buildings are houses of cards—literally. Bryan has captured the Guinness World Record at least ten times since 1992 for building the world's tallest house of cards. His most recent Guinness record was a 25-foot-tall, 2,400-deck, 133-card-level-high house he made in Berlin. It weighed about 200 pounds and took Berg two weeks to complete. He never glues, tapes, bends, notches, or folds, and he never goes over budget, since his only building material is cards—and cheap ones at that. Berg claims that when it comes to building houses, the lower the quality cards, the better. (He's sounding more and more like a builder I know.) "Shitty cards are key," he says.

A 1997 graduate of Iowa State's architecture program and currently a special lecturer at Iowa State's College of Design, Berg began stacking the decks at the tender age of eight after watching his grandfather stack cards for fun. And Berg kept on stacking them, buying whole cases of cards at a time from his hometown Hy-Vee in

Spirit Lake and moving ever closer to the ceiling of the family's home. At the age of seventeen, before he had even earned his high school diploma, he broke his first Guinness World Record for freestanding card structures with a 14-foot tower. And it's more than likely that Berg is the only student in Iowa State history to completely fund his education by building with cards.

Now that Berg has made the big time, he has an agent, Omaha-based Dean Short, whose Dean Short Talent Service specializes in fair and festival acts such as Steve Trash, "who makes magic out of trash for educational fun," and Cousin Grumpy's Pork Chop Show (don't ask). Over the years at fairs, conventions, and festivals around the world, Berg has made almost every structure imaginable, from pyramids to classic ballparks (including Philadelphia's Veterans Stadium and Brooklyn's Ebbetts Field) to the Empire State Building. He was even featured on *Ripley's Believe It or Not!* for his scale replica of the Iowa State Capitol at the 2000 Iowa State Fair.

So how does he do it? With gravity and patience, he'll quip. But if you really want to build like Berg, you're going to have to buy his 2003 book, *Stacking the Deck: Secrets of the World's Master Card Architect.* Coauthored by Berg and Thomas O'Donnell, former *Des Moines Register* reporter, the book gives you step-by-step instructions and lots of helpful illustrations for building your own card creations. So what to do when you accidentally knock down a towering card house, as you're sure to do many times? The master recommends staying calm, and he's learned how to do so himself the hard way—lots of experience. You might also consider stealing another page from Berg's book by breaking out the leaf blower to help clean up the mess.

None of Berg's work is on permanent display because it's liable to blow over. You can reach his agent, Dean Short, at (402) 553-3502 or visit www.cardstacker.com.

★ ★

Ever Meet a Wind Farmer?

Storm Lake

One of the world's biggest farms is located right here in northwest Iowa, but it doesn't produce a single pound of pork, gallon of milk, or bushel of corn or soy. And it's harvest time year-round on this farm, twenty-four hours a day, seven days a week. (Sounds like a farmer's worst nightmare.)

Dedicated in 1999, the Storm Lake wind-power facility is one of the largest wind-generated power facilities in the world. With 262 wind turbines spread over hundreds of acres between Cherokee and Buena Vista Counties, the facility generates 650,000 megawatt-hours of clean electricity, enough to fulfill the energy needs of about 64,000 average Midwestern homes—that is, those without three or more teenagers living inside. Each wind turbine is composed of

A windmill arm for the twenty-first century.

a tower (vaguely resembling a high-tension electrical tower) topped with three 79-foot blades. Weighing in excess of 5,300 pounds each, these blades are aerodynamically designed to produce lift much as an airplane wing does, so they only require an 8-mile-per-hour wind to turn them.

If you drive west on IA 7 out of Storm Lake, the wind turbines are visible to the north. The farmers make money by leasing the turbine land to the power company, the state gets some pollution-free energy, and drivers get something new to look at as they're cruising the back roads of Iowa. There's something slightly surreal about the rows and rows of turbines looming giantlike above the farmhouses and fields of corn, their 200-foot-high rotors spinning slowly in the wind. But the strangeness is all for a good cause: The wind farm helps keep thousands of tons of carbon dioxide and sulfur emissions out of our air (and lungs).

In Storm Lake you can find a single turbine blade from one of the towers (either that or it's a very long canoe). A present to the city from Enron, the power company that built the wind farm, the blade makes for a pretty striking town sculpture.

The turbine blade is located at the corner of Highway Street and East Lake Shore Drive, just east of downtown. Situated in both Buena Vista and Cherokee Counties, the wind farm is visible from IA 7 west of Storm Lake. For information about how to take a self-guided tour of the wind farm, go to www.stormlakechamber.com/attractions/windfarm.htm.

A Museum That Keeps Growing
Storm Lake

The Living Heritage Tree Museum, located in Sunset Park on the shores of Storm Lake, is an outdoor museum planted with fifty-one trees grown from seedlings and cuttings of trees associated with more or less famous people and events. One of my favorites is the Moon Tree, an American sycamore grown from a seed that was brought to the moon and back by crewmen of the *Apollo 12* flight. Come to think of it, the park is heavy on flight-associated people and events: There's a crabapple obtained from the home of Charles Lindbergh, who made the first solo flight across the Atlantic in 1927; a butternut from the Hamlin, West Virginia home of Chuck Yeager, who on October 14, 1947, became the first man to fly faster than the speed of sound; and a walnut descended from a tree that Orville and Wilbur Wright planted at their airfield outside of Dayton, Ohio.

One of the pleasures of the Living Heritage Tree Museum is wondering about the personality (or personalities) behind the tree selections. Stan Lemaster and Theodore Klein made the park possible by donating the heritage trees to Storm Lake. Lemaster, a retired General Electric computer engineer from Louisville, Kentucky, came up with the idea for heritage trees during a bout of insomnia.

Some of their selections are no-brainers, trees that anyone would want to have in their Living Heritage Tree Collection: a George Washington tulip poplar, an Abraham Lincoln white oak, a Ulysses S. Grant gum tree. But then there are a few surprises. How about the Ann Rutledge maple, grown from a maple shading the grave of Abraham Lincoln's alleged first sweetheart, whose death, according to the little plaque in front of the tree, was believed to be responsible for his melancholy disposition? Then there's the Colonel Harlan Sanders ash, from the home of Colonel Sanders in Shelbyville, Kentucky—yup, the same Colonel Sanders who became world-famous for his secret-recipe fried chicken. We can easily forgive Lemaster for playing local favorites, though.

The park also features some descendants of trees famous in their own right, including a Delicious apple tree, which originally grew by chance in Peru, Iowa, and was chopped down twice before owners figured out they had a good thing growing. Then there's an offspring of the Sir Isaac Newton apple tree, the famous tree that dropped a gravitational discovery right onto Newton's head. None of the trees are quite mature yet, though, so if you're looking to be struck with

★ ★

your own apple of insight, you're going to have to wait a while.

The Living Heritage Tree Museum is located in Sunset Park on West Lake Shore Drive, right on Storm Lake. Take West Fifth Street to Ontario Street, head south toward the lake, and the museum will be directly in front of you. Call (712) 732-3780 for more information.

One of the Many Eighth Wonders of the World
West Bend

The glossy tourist brochure for West Bend's Grotto of the Redemption makes the rather dubious but hard-to-refute claim that the structure is "frequently considered the Eighth Wonder of the World." Though it may or may not be among the world's top eight, or even top ten, wonders, the grotto definitely tops the list of Iowa wonders.

As large as a city block, more than 40 feet tall at its highest point, and composed of the largest collection of minerals and semiprecious stones in the world, the Grotto of the Redemption is both a shrine honoring the life of Jesus Christ and a monument to one man's obsession with rocks, minerals, and geodes. Father Paul Dobberstein began construction on the grotto as a young priest in 1912 and worked continuously on the project over the next four decades until his death in 1954. In the summertime he worked outdoors, building the grotto by hand, stone by stone, without the aid of machinery, save for an electric hoist that he purchased in 1947. During the long winter months, he built sections of the grotto indoors, carefully setting beautiful stones, minerals, shells, and corals into large sections of concrete.

In the spring and fall, Father Dobberstein traveled the country and the world in search of building materials for his ever-expanding shrine: agates from Brazil, Mexico, and Madagascar; azurite and malachite from the Ural Mountains of Russia; stalactites and stalagmites from caves in South Dakota and the Ozarks; pipe-organ coral from Hawaii; and amethysts from the Andes, to name just a sampling. All told, Dobberstein traveled more than 800,000 miles in his hunt for

Can you call four decades of grotto building a hobby? Catherine Cole

unique rocks and minerals, and experts now assess the geologic value of the grotto at more than $4 million. When, or if, he ever had time to give a sermon, marry a couple, or baptize a child, we haven't been able to ascertain.

The Grotto of the Redemption is, technically speaking, a conglomeration of nine separate grottos, or cavernlike structures, each one highlighting an important event in the life of Jesus, from his birth to his resurrection. Taking it all in is dizzying, to say the least. In addition to the concrete, rocks, and minerals, the grotto also contains colored glass, tile, shells of every shape and size, and petrified wood, all arranged in intricate patterns to create the structure's many

caves, arches, hollows, and stairways. The end result is a paradoxical ordered chaos. The grotto seems as much a work of nature as it does a man-made structure, with a roof that resembles mountain peaks shaped by wind and water instead of a builder's hand.

The grotto is flanked by the Grotto Park Restaurant, the Grotto Gift Shop, the Grotto Museum, and a beautiful Spanish Mission–style Catholic church (where Dobberstein would have presumably led his congregation in prayer if he hadn't been hunting for azurite and malachite from the Ural Mountains), complete with bell tower and red-tile roof. The museum contains a large display of some of the precious and semiprecious stones used in the construction of the grotto, as well as some early newspaper articles about Father Dobberstein and the shrine.

The Grotto of the Redemption is located in West Bend. Just follow the signs on IA 15 as you enter town. For more information or for group reservations, call (515) 887-2371 or (800) 868-3641 or visit www.westbendgrotto.com.

6

North Central

Ruth Rasmussen's World's *Largest Salt and Pepper Shaker Collection (well, it's second largest now, but who's counting?) is my personal favorite in North Central Iowa, but it's in the process of moving to a new home in a renovated building in Traer. Hopefully, it'll be safe and sound in its new digs soon. Arthur Peterson no longer gives tours of his five-story silo turned home, but you can drive by and have a look. The stuffed albino deer in its little display shed up in St. Ansgar, the 5,000-square-foot tree house in Marshalltown, and the World Largest Bullhead in Crystal Lake are all returning stars from the previous edition.*

Unfortunately, the house from the movie Twister *closed, along with the bed-and-breakfast and dirt racetrack there. And since the first edition, we've marked the fiftieth anniversary of the tragic deaths of Buddy Holly, Ritchie Valens, Jiles P. "the Big Bopper" Richardson, and their pilot, twenty-one-year-old Roger Peterson, in a cornfield just north of Clear Lake. Though a portion of it was stolen and then later replaced, the small memorial for the musicians is still at the crash site, with one addition: a stainless-steel monument in the form of pilot's wings to remember Roger Peterson.*

And one last change to note: The Kate Shelley High Bridge in Boone, a steel-trestle beauty that's the highest and longest double-track railroad bridge in the country, is soon to be replaced with a new concrete bridge that's almost as high but not nearly as pretty. It'll still be the longest and highest double-track in the country, though, and that counts for something.

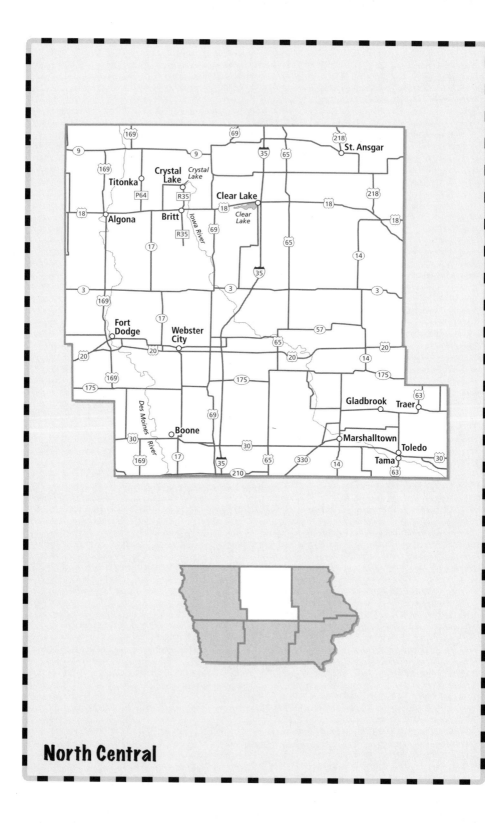

North Central

A Cheesy Attraction
Algona

In March of 2003 a man in Hawaii poured a single-serving bag of Cheetos into a bowl and out tumbled an unusually large morsel of cheesy, fried snack food that would forever change the history of one small Iowa town.

The man did what any red-blooded, technologically savvy American capitalist would do: He auctioned the Cheeto off on eBay, billing it as the world's largest. (Original reports called it "the size of a small lemon," though in actuality it's about as big as a chicken nugget.) His prospective sale caught the eyes of Internet-surfing folks across the country, including Bryce Wilson, a deejay in Algona looking for something to talk about on the air. He started a pledge drive to bring the Cheeto to town as a tourist attraction. Bryce said, "I got on the air that day and said, 'This is our chance! We're going to get ourselves on the map today! People will come from miles around! We'll need new roads just to accommodate all the traffic! It will be great for the economy!'" He raised $180.

In the meantime, online bidding for the Cheeto twice reached $99 million before eBay yanked it. Of course, no one had intentions of paying such a price, so the Cheeto's owner turned to his one serious offer, the community of Algona. He donated the Cheeto to the city, requesting that the $180 go to a local charity in his name.

News of the Cheeto's sale spread across the country, and the story was reported on Web sites, in newspapers, and on radio stations around the world, including CNN and a radio station in Australia. General Electric custom-made a bulletproof glass case for it. A New York glassblower blew a swirly orange pedestal for it. Locally, there was some controversy over the misshapen piece of snack food. Some thought the media stir ridiculous; others thought it just plain fun; and some even threatened to kidnap the Cheeto: C.L.A.M, the Cheeto Liberation Army of Men, as well as the women's organization, C.L.A.W., and one lone man calling himself Crouching Cheeto, Hidden HoHo.

★ ★

Iowa's most famous piece of overpuffed snack food. Clint Buckner

In the end, though, the Cheeto made it safely to its unveiling at Sister Sarah's Bar & Restaurant (thanks, in part, to a police and fire-truck escort). The national late-night TV talk show *Jimmy Kimmel LIVE* broadcast the event via satellite. Residents packed the place, wearing Cheeto T-shirts, hats, and jewelry. The mayor even gave a speech, declaring March 13 Giant Cheeto Day in Algona.

After the unveiling, much of the fervor died down. People still visit Sarah's specifically to see the Cheeto, which sits on a velvet pillow

on its custom-blown stand in its custom-made case on the mantel.
There are no T-shirts for sale, no signs outside of Sarah's, not even a
billboard anywhere in town. Its presence is requested in area parades
and at local high schools, but for the most part, it's back to business as usual in Algona. Bryce thinks it might be a few years before
residents are willing to embrace their new attraction wholeheartedly.
"Some people are kind of sick of it now, for obvious reasons," he
says. "But I'm quite happy to spread the joy of the Cheeto."

The World's Largest Cheeto is on display at Sister Sarah's Bar &
Restaurant in Algona. Take US 18 west off I-35 in Clear Lake, and
Sarah's is on the south side of the highway as you head into town.
Call (515) 295-7757 for more information.

German POWs Build Christmas Scene, Draw Crowds
Algona

One of Algona's star attractions, a sixty-piece, half-life-size Nativity
scene, can be visited only during the Christmas holiday season. This
was a specific request made by German prisoner of war Eduard Kaib,
who built the scene because he missed his family while he was at a
base camp near Algona in 1944.

During the Second World War, there were prison camps in most
states, and this one—with an average of 3,000 prisoners, nearly the
population of Algona at the time—processed German POWs for
thirty-four branch camps in Minnesota, Iowa, and the Dakotas. Were
they located here, smack-dab in the middle of the country, because
the absence of an ocean lent no hope of escape? Because Iowa men
fighting overseas had farmland that needed attention and prisoners
were cheap labor? Because the vice president at the time, Henry Wal-
lace, was an Iowan concerned with the economic and labor needs of
his home state? No one seems to know for sure, but it's estimated
that this particular camp system's prisoners completed about $3.5
million worth of work.

The prisoners were treated well. They had an orchestra, a chorus, and a dramatic club. They had canteen accounts that were credited 80 cents a day for their labor, with which they bought things like magazine subscriptions and sports equipment. Eduard Kaib, an architect and noncommissioned officer of the German army, bought building materials.

Eduard especially missed his home and family during the Christmas holidays, and so set about building a Nativity scene as a way to cure his loneliness. Five other POWs helped him. Over the course of a year, they hand-carved plaster set upon heavy concrete-covered wood-and-wire frames for all sixty pieces of the scene, from the baby Jesus and the Wise Men to sheep and camels. The project was completed in 1945, and when the camp was disbanded in 1946, Eduard left the scene in Algona, with three requests: that it stay in Algona, that there never be an admission charge to view it, and that it be viewed only at Christmastime.

His requests have been honored. Each December, thousands of people visit the scene in its own climate-controlled building at the local fairgrounds. Visitors have come from all fifty states and around the world. Eduard (now deceased) even returned once, and Algona residents gave him a grand reception. He came during the Christmas holiday season of 1968, and he brought his family.

Algona's Nativity scene can be viewed for free in December at the Kossuth County Fairground, located south of Algona at US 169 and Fair Street. Open Monday through Saturday from 2:00 to 9:00 p.m. and Sundays and Christmas Day from noon to 9:00 p.m.; special showings and tour groups on request. For more information, call the First United Methodist Men's Club at (515) 295-7241 or the Algona Area Chamber of Commerce at (515) 295-7201 or visit www .pwcamp.algona.org.

★ ★

Kate Shelley's Midnight Heroics

Boone

The story of Kate Shelley's heroics sounds like something straight out of Hollywood: late evening, torrential rains and a violent thunderstorm, a washed-out railroad bridge, and Kate, the seventeen-year-old heroine, crawling on her hands and knees across a 671-foot-long railroad bridge to save the midnight express and its 200 passengers from a tragic fate. Quite fittingly, she was rewarded with everything from a free lifetime pass on the railroad to the honor of having a very impressive bridge named after her, the Kate Shelley High Bridge, located just west of Boone, the longest and highest double-track railroad bridge in the country.

The more detailed story goes like this: Kate Shelley, her mother, and her four younger siblings (Kate's father died when she was only fourteen) lived in a small house on the banks of Honey Creek, right beside the railroad bridge. On July 6, 1881, a fierce rainstorm caused flooding, which threatened the Shelley's barn and home. The storm raged on into the night, and Kate and her mom stayed up to keep watch on the swollen creek as the younger children slept. Some time before midnight they heard a tremendous crunching sound as the bridge over Honey Creek, weakened by the floodwaters, gave way beneath a pusher engine with a crew of four, sent from Moingona to test the tracks as far as Boone.

Kate knew the Chicago-bound midnight express, due to pass from the west over first the Des Moines River Bridge and then the now washed-out Honey Creek Bridge, had to be stopped. In the thunder and lightning and torrential rain, she set out with a lantern for Moingona to alert the stationmaster. Though the station house was only a mile away, in between was the 50-foot-high Des Moines River Bridge, the raging floodwaters just yards below the tracks. Its cross ties were laid almost 3 feet apart to discourage people from walking across it. So Kate crawled. From timber to timber, an extinguished lantern clutched tightly in her hand, the flood-swollen waters of the Des Moines roaring

A little lady who deserved to have a
big bridge named after her.

below her, the powerful storm winds threatening to topple her from the bridge, Kate crawled the 671 perilous feet on her hands and knees. When she finally made it to the Moingona station, she was so exhausted that her speech was nearly incomprehensible. The men at the station reportedly thought she had gone crazy, but then they understood: "Stop the express—the Honey Creek Bridge is down!"

After the deed, Kate weathered a media onslaught and didn't get out of bed for thirty days. She received gifts of money and goods from passengers, the State of Iowa ($200), and the Chicago-Northwestern Railroad ($100, a half barrel of flour, half a load of coal, a gold watch, and a lifetime pass), and was offered free tuition at Simpson College in Indianola, where she planned to study to become a teacher. In 1903, after teaching for a number of years in Boone County, Kate was offered the job of stationmaster at Moingona, the very site of her heroics, and she served there until 1910, receiving so many visitors requesting her autograph and photo that she had hundreds of postcards of herself made up, which she sold, according to one report, "at a very small profit."

Located a few miles west of Boone and just a stone's throw away from the now-abandoned bridge Kate crossed that fateful night back in 1881, the Kate Shelley High Bridge, a steel-beam structure 186 feet high and stretching over a half mile between bluffs along the Des Moines River, looks far more Western than Midwestern. Completed in 1901, the bridge has been in operation for more than a hundred years and still sees quite a bit of traffic, an average of fifty trains a day. The Boone and Scenic Valley Railroad even offers a daily 12-mile trip in vintage 1920s rail cars, offering a breathtaking view of the bridge and the Des Moines River valley.

The old railway station at Moingona where Kate worked is now the site of the Kate Shelley Railroad Museum and Park. You can learn more about Kate's life there—not an easy one, in spite of the generosity of those so impressed by her bravery—and you can even buy postcards of the heroine, sold at a very small profit, of course. Kate Shelley would have approved.

★ ★

For more information about the Kate Shelley Railroad Museum, located at 1198 232nd Street in Moingona, call (515) 432-1907. The Kate Shelley High Bridge is 3 miles west of Boone on J Avenue. A replacement bridge (this one made of concrete) is being built beside it and is scheduled for completion sometime in 2009. (Even though it will be a little less high than the old High Bridge, it'll still be pretty high, and still retain the title of highest double-track trestle in the United States.) Follow Eighth Street west to the T intersection with Marion Avenue. Take a right onto Marion, cross the railroad tracks, and then take a left onto 198th Road. Follow the signs to the Kate Shelley High Bridge.

For more information about the Boone & Scenic Valley Railroad, located at 225 Tenth Street in Boone, call (800) 626-0319. The railroad offers weekday train rides over the bridge at 1:30 p.m. and twice-daily weekend and holiday rides at 1:30 p.m. and 4:00 p.m.

Convention Dress Code: Railroad Casual
Britt

A quick run through the National Hobo Convention in Britt could leave you wondering why present-day hobos look eerily like residents of a small Iowa town. But Britt's hobos are actually residents of this small Iowa town; after all, the convention is their celebration.

And the hobos are there (look for characteristic railroad touches such as overalls, train-conductor hats, bandanas, and backpacks). They're just heavily outnumbered by the residents, which makes sense considering that the number of hobos nationwide has dwindled to a few hundred (down from a few hundred thousand during the hobo heyday of the Great Depression). But these wandering rail-riders still do exist, believe it or not, and though there are hobo conventions throughout the country, this one, started in 1900, is the granddaddy of them all. The town is also home to a hobo foundation, the country's only hobo museum, and the world's only hobo memorial.

Can someone tell me where to find the panel discussion on advances in campfire cooking? Clint Buckner

Hobos and residents alike gather here annually during the second weekend in August for rickety carnival rides, a flea market, museum tours, free mulligan stew, and the crowning of the king and queen of the hobos. Stretch and Connecticut Tootsie won the 2008 election, which was held under the city park pavilion and decided, as usual, by applause. The two will spend the next year traveling the country (a given, really, considering they're hobos), promoting Britt and the national convention.

After one election in 2003, Hobo King Spike caught his breath behind the counter at the Hobo Museum, when a woman with her son, who had never seen a real live hobo before, spied his bandana. "You're a hobo, aren't you?" she asked. The answer came, better than she could have dreamed: "I'm the king of the hobos," he said proudly. The wide-eyed boy went back to meet the king, and the mingling of hobos and non-hobos at this historic hobo gathering continued.

The National Hobo Convention takes place the second week in August in Britt, located west of Clear Lake on US 18. For more information, contact the Britt Chamber of Commerce at (641) 843-3867 or visit www.brittiowa.com.

Groovin' at the Surf
Clear Lake

The Surf Ballroom is famous for being the venue where Buddy Holly, Ritchie Valens, and Jiles P. "the Big Bopper" Richardson played their last show before dying in a plane crash in a farmer's field 5 miles north of town. For visitors primarily interested in the so-called Day the Music Died, there's a stone monument to the trio just outside the Surf as well as a memorial inside that fills quite a few feet of wall space, including large photographs of Valens, Holly, and Richardson; posters advertising the fateful Winter Dance Party on February 2, 1959; newspaper articles; and more.

But if you venture past the memorial, you'll find there's quite a bit more to the Surf than the story of the events of that tragic night. For starters, the Surf is a true rarity, an authentic ballroom from the heyday of the Big Bands that looks as if it's passed through the years unchanged. High vaulted ceilings, beautiful hardwood floors, booths against the walls of the main dance hall, tables beside the dance floor—all the nightclub details feel so familiar (either from your past if you're a certain age or from movies if you're a lot younger than a certain age) that stepping out onto the Surf's 6,300-square-foot dance floor feels like a strange sort of homecoming. If you want to take a more detailed trip down memory lane, the Surf's Hall of Fame contains photos, autographs, and other memorabilia from the Big Band era. And be sure to check the wall backstage for the signatures of past performers at the Surf.

The way rock 'n' roll used to be.

Though the Surf is located just across the street from Clear Lake, there really isn't any surf to speak of, across the road or even within 1,000 miles of the club's doors. But in the service of good old-fashioned escapism, the Surf was designed to resemble a South Seas beach club, with puffy white clouds on the ceiling and oceanfront murals behind the main stage and along the walls, featuring long stretches of sandy beach, palm trees, sailboats, and, of course, some foamy surf. Did someone say piña colada?

The Surf, located at 460 North Shore Drive, is open to the public from 8:00 a.m. to 4:00 p.m. daily and plays host to a variety of rock 'n' roll, jazz, blues, and Big Band acts throughout the year. For more information, including a schedule of events, call (641) 357-6151 or visit www.surfballroom.com.

The Field Where the Music Died

In the early morning of February 3, 1959, the plane carrying Buddy Holly, Ritchie Valens, Jiles P. "the Big Bopper" Richardson, and pilot Roger Peterson crashed in a farmer's field 5 miles north of Clear Lake and came to rest along a fencerow. Even though the exact spot went unmarked for many years, fans of the trio still walked into the cornfields to pay their respects and leave flowers and other mementos. But according to Ken Paquette, a fan from Portersfield, Wisconsin, because there was no memorial, people didn't know exactly where to pay their respects and where to leave their offerings. "People really weren't sure where it was," he said, "and I thought there should be something there."

So in honor of the three musicians he built a small stainless-steel monument composed of a guitar engraved with their names along with three stainless-steel 45s, each one engraved with the title of one of their hit songs: Holly's "Peggy Sue," Valens's "Donna," and the Big Bopper's "Chantilly Lace." And now that people know where to leave their "gifts," there's no shortage of odd stuff at the site. Surrounding the monument when we visited were faded plastic flowers, lightly coated with dust; some coins (mostly pennies) scattered on the ground; six lighters; twelve pens; a faded Cubs cap; too many business cards to count, including one from a policeman in Fort Madison and one from a tire salesman in Sioux City; a health-insurance card from Connecticut; an American Airlines Advantage card; a couple of wallet-size family portraits; seven or eight large, cloth-covered elastic ponytail holders; and a card from a local corn maze with a start time of 5:05 p.m. and a finish time of 5:31 p.m.

Holly arranged for the private flight out of Mason City Airport after enduring a brutally cold trip across Iowa on a tour bus that had developed heating-system problems; it was reported that one drummer even got frostbite. He and his two backup musicians, Waylon Jennings (yup, the same Waylon Jennings who later became a country-and-western sensation) and Tommy Allsup, would travel to the next show in comfort, and with the time they gained on the rest of the musicians, the group planned to do their laundry (even stars have to wash their socks). After hearing that the Big Bopper was running a fever, presumably from the bus ride from hell, Jennings graciously gave up his seat on the flight. When Holly heard Jennings wasn't going to fly, he said to him, "Well, I hope your old bus freezes up." Without missing a beat Waylon Jennings replied, "Well, I hope your plane crashes." (Jennings reportedly relived that brief exchange for years.) Tommy Allsup offered to flip Ritchie Valens for the remaining seat and, in losing the coin toss, saved his own life.

Investigators never determined the precise cause of the crash, though they speculated that inclement weather—a light dusting of snow fell that night—and pilot error were contributing factors. The deaths of three hit musicians prompted newspapers to call the tragedy "The Day the Music Died," and Don McLean later memorialized the trio, and the phrase, in his hit song "American Pie." The plaintive melancholy of that song perfectly matches the loneliness and isolation of the spot where the plane that carried Holly, Valens, Richardson, and pilot Roger Peterson came to rest, beside a fence in a field of corn miles outside of town.

The field where the music died.

Ken Paquette added another monument to the site in February 2009, the fiftieth anniversary of the crash, this one in the shape of pilot's wings to honor the twenty-one-year-old pilot, Roger Peterson. From US 18 in Clear Lake, go north on North Eighth Street for 4.7 miles. When the road starts to curve left, take a right onto 310th Street, a gravel road, and then take the first left onto Gull Avenue. Follow Gull Avenue north for about half a mile, just past the grain bins to the first fencerow. There's space to park on the right side of the road. Walk west along the fencerow for about half a mile until you reach the memorial.

Pyramid for Rent

Clear Lake

If you happen to be in the market for a short-term pyramid rental in north-central Iowa but just haven't found what you're looking for, look no more. The Pyramid House, located just across the street from 3,600-acre Clear Lake, one of the largest spring-fed lakes in Iowa, is available for both weekly and monthly rentals. Though the Pyramid House is definitely on the smallish side for a pyramid—with 5,500 square feet of space and a height of only about 37 feet, it's downright puny compared to the 482-foot-high, thirteen-acre Great Pyramid in Egypt—it's a pretty spacious lake rental. And with five bedrooms, three bathrooms, and a two-and-a-half-car garage, you can bring your kids, your friends, and your friends' kids, as well as that half car you rarely get to drive, and make a week of it.

One of the house's strong points (besides the actual one on top) are the many large windows looking south onto the lake; almost every room fills with sunlight and offers a beautiful view. Other

A little bit of Egypt in Iowa.

features include two decks, Italian marble floors, and a long dock across the street for sunbathing and swimming. And if you tire of the sun and water or if the rain comes, the Surf Ballroom, Clear Lake's famous music venue, is just a few blocks down the street. Don't even bother checking the basement for sarcophagi, though. Either there never were any, or they were in violation of code and the rental inspectors made the owners haul them away.

The Pyramid House is located at 1102 North Shore Drive. Both weekly and monthly rentals are available. For rates and additional information, call (515) 987-7441 or visit www.mypyramidhouse.com.

A Genuine Reproduction of a Famous Fake
Fort Dodge

Fort Dodge is the original home of the Cardiff Giant, a 10-foot-tall statue with 21-inch feet that has been called "the greatest hoax in history." We say his *original* home because Old Hoaxey, as nineteenth-century fans started calling him, was sculpted from a massive five-ton block of Fort Dodge gypsum. And even though the original Cardiff Giant resides at the Farmer's Museum in Cooperstown, New York, Fort Dodge is still home to the Cardiff Giant, or one of the Cardiff giants. (There are four that we know about, but there could be many, many more.) You can visit him, or a re-creation of him, at the Fort Museum, a re-creation (sense a pattern here?) of the fort built in 1862 to protect local residents from Indian raids.

The story of the Cardiff Giant is as intriguing as a soap opera love affair. George Hull, an atheist cigarmaker from Binghamton, New York, reportedly came up with the idea after arguing with a revivalist minister about the absurdity of a biblical passage referring to antediluvian giants: "There were giants in the earth in those days" (Genesis 6:4). Hull traveled to Fort Dodge; ordered a five-ton gypsum block to go (claiming he needed the stone for patriotic statuary); oversaw the sculpting and aging process in Chicago of a giant, supine man, hips canted, right arm draped across his chest; and then buried the statue

A Big One That Can't Get Away

Weighing in at around 1,650 pounds and with a total nose-to-tail-tip length of some 17 feet 8 inches, Crystal Lake's famed bull-head is a fish that even the most unscrupulous teller of fish tales could be honest about. "He must have weighed almost two tons," he could say, without batting an eye. "As big as Shamu at Sea World and a whole lot uglier, too. Could have swallowed me and Ed whole and still had room left over to down the cooler of beer for dessert." And every word of it would be true.

The statue, hailed as the World's Largest Bullhead, was built in 1958, and ever since then it's served as a town mascot, prime snapshot spot, and mighty tough yardstick (or five and a half yardsticks, to be more exact) by which locals might measure their own angling achievements.

The World's Largest Bullhead is located at the end of Main Street on the shore of 263-acre Crystal Lake.

at his brother-in-law William "Stub" Newell's farm in Cardiff, New York, a region already known for its fossils.

About a year later on Saturday, October 16, 1869, Stub Newell hired workmen to dig a well in the exact spot where he and Hull had buried the giant; about 3 feet down, they struck one of his huge feet and then quickly set about uncovering all 10 feet. Word of the "discovery" quickly spread, and soon hundreds of people were visiting Newell's farm every day, paying 50 cents apiece for a look at what some speculated was the petrified body of a member of the ancient race of giants mentioned in Genesis.

On October 23, Stub Newell, acting on Hull's behalf, sold a three-fourths interest in the giant to five local businessmen for $30,000, a very healthy return on Hull's $2,600 investment. In order to accommodate larger crowds, the group moved the giant to Syracuse, where press attention and speculation about his origins intensified. One expert, Dr. John F. Boynton, rejected the antediluvian giant theory and hypothesized that it was a statue created by a seventeenth-century Jesuit missionary to awe local Indian tribes. Still, the crowds of giant-lovers kept coming.

By November, though, the hoax started to unravel. Farmers in the area reported having seen a very large crate being unloaded at the Newell farm, and a Yale paleontologist, Othniel C. March, citing fresh chisel marks, pronounced the giant a "decided humbug of recent origin." On December 10 Hull came clean, but at that point, it didn't seem to matter. The crowds were still coming, and still paying, to see the fake from Fort Dodge. P. T. Barnum even offered $60,000 to rent the giant for a three-month circus stint, but the group had already decided to take him on the road themselves and refused. Barnum commissioned a fake of the fake, made of wood and covered in plaster, and when the original fake and the facsimile of the fake were displayed that December in New York City just two blocks apart, the Barnum fake reportedly outdrew the original. Tough crowd.

Just in case you want to make a road trip, you can visit the original Barnum fake at Marvin's Marvelous Mechanical Museum in Farmington Hills, Michigan; or, if you're interested in seeing a fake of Barnum's fake of Hull's fake, you can visit Circus World in Baraboo, Wisconsin. But here in Fort Dodge, you can visit a fake of the original phony, made from the very same Fort Dodge gypsum. Think of him as the Cardiff giant's honest brother, a giant who never pretended to be anything other than what he was: a big fake.

The Fort Museum, which contains a complete frontier village as well as the Cardiff Giant replica, is located a quarter mile east of the intersection of US 169 and US 20. It's open mid-April through October. Monday through Saturday hours are 9:00 a.m. to 5:00 p.m., and Sunday it's open 11:00 a.m. to 5:00 p.m. For more information, call (515) 573-4231 or visit www.fortmuseum.com.

★ ★

Toothpick Anyone?
Gladbrook

Matchstick artist Patrick Acton's big breakthrough came a decade into his matchstick-model-building career: He called the Ohio Blue Tip Company, makers of blue-tip wooden matches, and discovered that, why yes, they'd be happy to sell him matchsticks without the sulfur tip. This might sound insignificant until you realize that Pat had been cutting the tip off of every single matchstick he used to build his models of everything from country churches to sailing ships. And a lot of matchsticks go into making a matchstick model. By the time he made his discovery, he had cut the tips off more than 100,000 of them. No use crying over cut matchsticks, though.

And that's when his matchstick model making really took off. Pat's total matchsticks per model went from hundreds to thousands, their dimensions ballooned, and it wasn't long before Ripley's Believe It or Not! started purchasing models to display in their museums all around the world, from Copenhagen to Key West. They've now bought a total of fifteen of Pat's stunning creations.

At the Matchstick Marvels Museum you'll find the USS *Nimitz* aircraft carrier, an impressive 40,000 matchsticks; the space shuttle *Challenger,* a remarkable 200,000 matchsticks; the U.S. Capitol, a mind-boggling 478,000 matchsticks; and a lot of others too. The models are exquisitely detailed, near-perfect renderings of buildings, boats, planes, and creatures, all in that lovely shade of toothpick. Currently Pat's hard at work on a stunning masterpiece, J. R. R. Tol-kien's fantastical City of Kings, which he predicts will contain over three million matchsticks.

Pat's discovered some fairly ingenious building techniques over the years, including a process whereby he glues a mat of matchsticks to Plexiglas, allows the glue to dry, and then peels the matchsticks off in one sheet. It's kind of like plywood made of matchsticks. But his real secret is pretty basic, he says: He glues one stick at a time.

The Matchstick Marvels Museum is open daily April through November from 1:00 to 4:00 p.m. For additional information, call (641) 473-2410 or visit www.matchstickmarvels.com.

A Tree House on Steroids

Marshalltown

Sometime in the early 1980s, then college junior Michael Jurgensen asked his grandparents if he could build a deck on the back of their house, 3 miles east of Marshalltown. Parents and grandparents take note: Michael's grandparents said no, so he decided to build a simple platform in the silver maple out back instead. Twenty-one summers and a whole lot of lumber and man-hours later, the tree house is now a twelve-level, 55-foot-tall, 5,000-square-foot behemoth, with a microwave, refrigerator, lights, phone, running water, and a pretty darn good sound system to boot. The Jurgensen house still doesn't have a deck.

Michael—or Mick, as his friends call him—showed an interest in all things mechanical from an early age. For his fifth birthday he asked his grandparents for 500 feet of speaker wire for a little home-sound-system project. Now in his forties and a local elementary-school principal and music teacher, Mick still has a lot of enthusiasm for his experiment in arboreal architecture. "I've never had a plan for it," he said. "I just get excited about doing something new and wait for the next idea to come. When I start sketching and actually see it on paper, I know it's going to happen." It appears Mick has done an awful lot of sketching over the years, and more additions and improvements are surely brewing.

The tree house has grown so big that it's evolved into a wooden superstructure interlaced between the tree's large branches and dense foliage. There are rails and staircases between all levels except the eleventh and twelfth (you need to climb a ladder to get to the very top), but the whole structure is open, and with fourteen porch

swings as well as numerous benches and picnic tables, there are lots of spots to sit and enjoy the great views. There are so many nooks and crannies that it seems you could spend the whole day exploring the shady decks Mick's spent the last two decades building.

The Big Tree House is located at the Jurgensens' Shady Oaks Campground, which, when it opened in 1925, was the first cabin camp west of the Mississippi on the Lincoln Highway. Shaded by a grove of 200-year-old burr oaks, the campground is a beautiful spot to enjoy the ninety-seven channels on your RV's satellite TV. And should reruns get you down, you can retire to the Big Tree House, sit on a porch swing, and contemplate the questionable wisdom of saying "no deck" to an ambitious youngster.

To get to Shady Oaks Campground and the Big Tree House, take US 30 west out of Marshalltown for 3 miles. Turn left onto Shady Oaks Road, and the tree house will be a quarter mile down the road on the left. Though the tree house is Mick's labor of love, his grandmother Mary Gift serves as tour guide, and visits are by appointment only. For more information or to make an appointment, call (641) 752-2946 or visit www.bigtreehouse.net/treehouse.html.

A Deer in Need of Sunscreen and Some Good Camo
St. Ansgar

"Albino animals tend not to survive long because they have no camouflage, no way to hide from predators," says Guy Zenner of the Iowa Department of Natural Resources. "From a biological perspective it's a defect." Try telling that to the folks up in St. Ansgar, though, and you'll make some enemies mighty quick. During the 1980s an all-white deer living a few miles outside of town became the town's de facto mascot and most famous citizen. Not only did they lobby the Iowa legislature to prohibit the taking of predominantly white white-tailed deer, they also stuffed and enshrined their own albino doe (after she died of natural causes, of course) in a cedar, glass-enclosed gazebo in the center of town.

St. Ansgar's albino deer was born in the spring of 1980 and, though biologically at risk, lived for eight and a half years within a 4-mile radius of where she was born. According to the plaque at her hooves, she gave birth to fifteen fawns, all normal color, and died in the winter of 1988 of pneumonia, kidney failure, and old age. (She also complained of aching joints, some memory and hearing loss, and constipation, in spite of all the good roughage in her diet.) Over the course of her long life, she became a town celebrity. The newspaper periodically wrote updates about her doings, families made trips to the fields at dusk to see if they could catch a glimpse of her feeding with her fawns, and a group of St. Ansgar citizens were instrumental in getting the Iowa legislature to help protect albino white-tailed deer from hunters.

And, of course, after she died, town residents chipped in for a full-body mount and displayed her first at the Heartland Power Cooperative and then downtown in a small park right across from Village Hardware. She stands—head tilted slightly to the left, pink eyes gazing at the building across the street—in a rectangular glass case inside a glass-enclosed cedar gazebo with a little cupola on top. Inside there's a plaque giving the bare facts of her life, some fake snow and dried cornhusks on the floor to give the scene a wintry look, framed documents signed by Governor Bransted having some-thing to do with the albino-deer-protection legislation, and two 8-by-12-inch photographs of the deer standing in winter fields, corn stubble at her feet.

It's no accident St. Ansgar chose flattering winter scenes to display their beloved albino deer. In spring, summer, and fall, a white coat might not be the best camouflage, but it's certainly no liability during the long northern Iowa winters.

St. Ansgar's albino deer can be found downtown across from Vil-lage Hardware at the corner of Fourth and Mitchell.

Bank Robbers Run Short-Lived Taxi Service

Picture this scene: A female employee is in a room on the upper floor of a bank that is being robbed by armed men. She goes to a window and looks out onto a back alley, hoping to find someone, anyone who can help. Standing below her at the bank's back entrance is a short, thick-necked man dressed in a dark suit. "We're being robbed!" she shouts. "The bank is being robbed!" The man slowly turns and, looking up at her, brandishes a machine gun. In a calm, gruff voice he says, "You're telling me, lady?"

Though it sounds like a scene from a Quentin Tarantino film, it really happened, right in downtown Mason City at the height of the Great Depression. The bank was the First National Bank, the man in the alley was Lester "Baby Face Nelson" Gillis, and the thug running the show inside was John Dillinger, the notorious gangster from Indiana. From September 1933 until July 1934, Dillinger and his gang terrorized the Midwest, robbing banks and police arsenals and staging three jail breaks (Dillinger himself broke out of jail using a fake wooden gun only ten days before the Mason City robbery), killing ten men and wounding seven others along the way.

On March 13, 1934, Dillinger, Baby Face Nelson, Homer Van Meter, Eddie Green, Tommy Carroll, and John Hamilton hit Mason City's First National Bank. The gang had hoped to net more than $240,000, a huge sum of money at the time, but due to a number of complications—not least of which was the fact that a bold teller named Harry Fisher kept passing Hamilton stacks of $1 bills instead of the larger denominations he demanded—they made off with only about $52,000. Dillinger's hopes to use his share of the big payoff to leave the country were dashed. He was shot and killed by FBI agents a little more than four months later, on July 22, outside the Biograph Theater in Chicago.

No one was killed in the robbery, but both Dillinger and Hamilton received shoulder wounds, and one bystander was shot and wounded, by either Hamilton or Baby Face Nelson, depending on the account you happen to read. What is certain is that to make their getaway, the gangsters used Mason City citizens as human shields. According to reports, they gathered hostages from the bank to ride the running boards of their Packard as they fled. Anne Youngdale recalled that Dillinger took three of her mother's bridge-playing "lady friends" for a ride far out into the countryside. "He put them all tied up on the running boards so he wouldn't be shot," she said. "What a ride! The ladies were released way out in nowhere." Reportedly, as the group passed

A bank that wasn't such an easy target.

slowly through town (the car could go only 15 miles per hour because of all the weight), an elderly hostage named Miss Minnie Piehm called out, "Let me out! This is where I live!" And Dillinger let her off. Next stop, nowhere!

The First National Bank is located in downtown Mason City at the corner of State and Federal Streets.

★ ★

Iowa's Nineteenth-, Twentieth-, and Twenty-First-Century Indian Entrepreneurs
Tama

After the Black Hawk War of 1832, a sort of last stand for Native Americans along the Mississippi, a series of Indian land cessions in Iowa between 1832 and 1845 left tribes like the Meskwaki (also known as the Fox tribe) without any land at all. The government forced the removal of the Meskwaki to a reservation in northeastern Kansas in 1845, and of the 1,227 tribe members who made the journey from east-central Iowa, fewer than half survived due to an epidemic of smallpox.

Sounds like a familiar tale, no? But wait, the story actually takes a turn for the better. Around 300 Meskwaki Indians remained behind, refusing to leave. Within a few years, other tribe members returned from Kansas, and the group lived quietly along the banks of the Iowa River for ten years before the state passed a law "allowing" the Meskwaki to stay. (I don't think they were planning on going anywhere.) Then, on July 13, 1857, the Iowa Meskwaki purchased their first eighty acres in Tama County along the banks of the Iowa. (The only reason the seller did business with the Meskwaki was greed: They were willing to pay $1,000 for the parcel, nearly ten times what a white man had to pay.) The Meskwaki once again had a homeland.

And the homeland grew. Each year between 1857 and 1866, the tribe purchased more acreage by trading trees, horses, and furs. In 1867 the United States finally began paying the tribe annuities for the land it had stolen, excuse us, "bought," back in the 1830s for about 10 cents an acre, and the Indian land purchases grew in size. By 1901 the Meskwaki had amassed 3,000 acres, and by 1987 the tribe owned outright a total of 7,054 acres of land in the center of the state of Iowa.

With a tribal enrollment of over 1,000 people, the Meskwaki community is now a vital part of the economic and cultural life in Tama County. They opened a 127,669-square-foot casino, with four

An old photo of a Meskwaki tribe member in traditional dress. Catherine Cole

restaurants and an attached 208-room hotel, which employs more than 1,000 people. And each August, on the original eighty-acre parcel it bought over 150 years ago, the tribe holds the Meskwaki Powwow, a four-day-long event based historically on a ceremony called the Green Corn Dance, during which the community came together to visit, rest, and celebrate the harvest. Persons outside the community are welcome to attend the ceremonial dances along the Iowa River. According to tribe historian Jonathan Buffalo, though, inviting those outside the tribe has been a rather recent development. And with a history like theirs, who can blame the Meskwaki for being a little cautious about inviting the neighbors?

225

★ ★

The Meskwaki casino and settlement are located just south of Tama off US 63. The casino is at 1504 305th Street. For general information, call (641) 484-2108; for information about the Meskwaki Powwow, held each year in mid-August, call (641) 484-4678 or (641) 484-5358 or visit www.meskwaki.org.

Silo Penthouse w/View
Titonka

You've probably heard of barns being converted into designer, exposed-beam homes, but what about moving the whole family into the silo out back? Just think of all that great space wasted on feed. And think of all the things a Midwestern Martha Stewart could do with a 40-foot-tall metal cylinder, a charge card, and a little imagination.

If you want an example of how to turn a silo into a home, complete with penthouse on top, then you need look no farther than northern Iowa. Arthur "Hap" Peterson built his silo home—the only one in the state, as far as we can tell—back in 1983. He bought a new Madison silo for the project, fitted it with specially constructed metal frames for the windows, and then built four floors inside. The ground level features a laundry, half-bath, and office; the second floor a family and entertainment room; the third floor a bedroom and full bath; and the fourth the kitchen and dining room. To top it all off, Hap built a wooden penthouse on the ground, with six picture windows and a true wraparound porch, and then raised the structure to the top of the silo by crane. The end architectural effect is truly notable, a cross between giant agricultural scepter and Midwestern lighthouse.

Titonka is on CR P64 (formerly called State Route 226), north of US 18. The silo home is located just southeast of town at 3201 220th Avenue. Arthur Peterson no longer gives tours, but you can still drive by and see it from the road.

A Butter Sculpture in Bronze

Toledo

Duffy knows cows: Jersey, Guernsey, Holstein, Milking Shorthorn, Ayrshire, Brown Swiss. You name your favorite Iowa ruminant, and she knows it by heart (and by hand). Not only is Norma "Duffy" Lyons a dairy farmer with a 1,300-acre operation in Toledo, she also happens to be the woman who sculpted the Iowa State Fair's butter cow for forty-six years, from 1960 to 2005. "I can sculpt any dairy breed you can think of off the top of my head," she says matter-of-factly. And for proof, you needed to look no further than her life-size butter cows. If they weren't colored a low-moisture, pure-cream-Iowa-butter yellow, you'd think they were entries in the livestock show.

Lyons achieved these remarkable results with some rather messy materials and less-than-pleasant working conditions. She'd start by softening about 600 pounds of frozen butter at room temperature, most of which was recycled from last year's butter cow. (They started recycling after the sponsors griped about how pricey butter was by the half ton.) Once the butter thawed enough to be worked, she would apply it to a wood-and-wire-mesh frame built into the vague shape of a cow, starting at the head and neck and then working her way down the body. Oh, and did we mention the whole sculpting process takes place in a 42-degree cooler?

But Duffy didn't just know cows. She also did some impressive butter sculptures of other subjects, and part of the anticipation surrounding each state fair was (and still is) the question of what's going to be sculpted next in butter. Lyons made creamy versions of everyone from Charlie Brown to Elvis to Garth Brooks to Jesus and his apostles, all of which drew fair-goers by the thousands.

Toledo commissioned a bronze cow and calf from Duffy for display in town, and her sculptures have been displayed at county and state fairs in thirteen states and in Canada. She's been the subject

of countless radio, newspaper, and magazine stories (both local and national), and appeared on the *Today Show* and *Late Night with David Letterman*. Maybe it's the firm-footed farmer in her, but Duffy doesn't seem too impressed by any of it. "I've been on the Letterman show. He flew me out to New York, bought one seat for me and one for a cow I molded out of cheese. It was okay, I guess." It's pretty tough to impress Duffy Lyons, but somehow impressing Iowans year after year came second nature to her.

In 2006 Duffy passed the butter—and butter sculpting—to Sarah Pratt of West Des Moines, but not before Pratt served a fifteen-year apprenticeship. And even though she's got big hoofprints to follow, Pratt's already a new favorite at the state fair.

Duffy's bronze cow and calf is located at the northwest junction of US 63 and US 30 in Toledo. For details, call (641) 484-6661. The Iowa State Fair is held each August at the Iowa State Fair Grounds just off I-80 in Des Moines. Take I-80 to exit 141 (US 65), and then take US 65 south to exit 79. Follow University Avenue west to the fairgrounds. For more information about the fair, call (800) 545-3247 or visit www.iowastatefair.org.

More Shakers Than You Can Shake a Stick At
Traer

Ruth Rasmussen may seem like a typical Iowa grandmother: She's got white hair, she knits, and she's just about the most hospitable and welcoming woman you'll ever meet. But she also has the Guinness-record-book-certified second-largest (it used to be first) collection of salt and pepper shakers in the world, as well as enough dogged determination and independence to remind you that this was once a land of pioneers.

If collecting 14,000 of anything isn't proof enough of iron will, just listen to Mrs. Rasmussen speak. She's fond of saying "I don't care," with a devilish twinkle in her eye, as in, I don't care what

The easiest grandmother in the world to shop for—
another salt and pepper shaker set it is! Catherine Cole

people think. "People tell me I should sell them and take the money. But I don't care—I want to keep them." She'll say it again when you notice her recumbent (and headless) nude-woman shakers, with the salt in one detachable breast and pepper in the other. "People say, 'Oh, what are you doing with that one?' but I don't care."

When she kept the collection at her home in two big sheds around back, there was a small sign in front of her house, and if you knocked on the door, she'd take you around back and give you a tour. Plans are currently under way to move the collection downtown

and turn it into a Salt and Pepper Shaker Museum. ("I can't take care of all of them anymore," Ruth says.)

Someday soon you'll be able to see her mind-bogglingly diverse collection. She's got Empire State buildings; sumo wrestlers; ballerinas; cartoon characters; every kind of wild and domesticated animal, from cows to lions to very, very long dogs; commemorative shakers from Princess Di's wedding; all fifty states; and corn, corn, and more corn (this is Iowa after all). She's also got all the U.S. presidents, except for the current one—no prejudice there, she just hasn't gotten around to cutting out his portrait and pasting it onto a plain white shaker, as she had to do with Bush and Clinton before him, since the company that made presidential shakers went out of business.

One presidential highlight has to be the shaker with Bill and Hillary Clinton's heads bobbing back and forth atop the White House: Hillary shakes her head no, while Bill shakes his head yes. Who would have guessed there are shakers that deliver presidential political analysis as well as salt and pepper?

Ruth's Rasmussen's second-largest salt and pepper shaker collection in the world will soon be housed in a newly renovated building on the west end of Second Street in Traer. For updates on the museum's progress, you can contact Ellen Young at the Traer Chamber of Commerce at traerchamber@hotmail.com.

Need an Exotic Chick?
Webster City

Take out a pencil, put your books on the floor, and move your desk away from your neighbor's—we're having a pop chicken quiz. Yes, answers need to be in complete sentences. And we won't start until the young man in the back stops making the clucking noises.

- How can you tell if a hen will lay brown eggs or white eggs?
- Is it possible to tell whether an egg is fresh without cracking

Is that peeping I hear coming from the mailbox?

it open? If so, how does one go about determining an egg's freshness?

- Extra credit: What's the world's largest mail-order chick hatchery?

The answer to the extra-credit question is Murray McMurray Chicks, a rare-breed hatchery and mail-order chick company in Webster City, and the first two questions came directly from the list of frequently asked questions on McMurray's Web site (see answers below).

Murray McMurray started his chicken business back in 1917. He was in banking at the time, but he sold baby chicks through the bank to area farmers up until the early stages of the Depression, when his bank went bust. Then he decided to go into the hatchery and mail-order chick business full-time. And the rest, as they say in Webster City, is history.

For years McMurray Chicks was run out of a private residence at 609 Ohio Street, which had been converted to a hatchery, but not long ago they built a 24,000-square-foot facility that can hatch up to 100,000 chicks a week. Rare-breed varieties for sale include Buff Brahmas, with their dramatically feathered feet; White Crested Black Polish, featuring large white crests that resemble old-fashioned judges' wigs; Turkens, which have completely bare turkey-like necks; and Red Frizzle Cochins, with feathers that curve outward and forward, giving them the appearance of having just walked 5 miles backward into a stiff wind. Most chicks sell for around $3 apiece, but you need to order at least a dozen. McMurray ships them express and guarantees 100 percent live arrival at your door. (But since travel time can take two or three days, be prepared to receive some hungry, and noisy, chicks on your doorstep.)

Answers: So how can you tell if a hen will lay brown eggs or white, class? Check their earlobes. (What, you didn't know chickens had earlobes? And you call yourself a Midwesterner.) Chickens with red earlobes will lay brown eggs, whereas chickens with white earlobes will lay white ones. And how do you tell if an egg that you found in the henhouse after a week's vacation is fresh? Easy. Just set it in water. Fresh eggs haven't had time to absorb much air, so they sink; eggs that aren't so fresh float.

For homework, study the Murray McMurray Web site at www .mcmurrayhatchery.com. Tours aren't offered. Class dismissed.

index

index

index

index

index

index

index

index

about the authors

Eric Jones is an east coast transplant, having come to Iowa City to attend the University of Iowa's Nonfiction Writing Program. He currently works as a household mover, but he's open to other offers. This is his first book.

Dan Coffey is best known as public radio's Dr. Science. He was a cofounder of the comedy troupe called Duck's Breath Mystery Theater, which performed for twelve years in San Francisco. Coffey and fellow comedian Merle Kessler developed the *Ask Dr. Science* show, which has been a staple on public radio since 1983. Coffey now makes his home in Iowa City where he continues to write in a humorous vein.

Contributor Berit Thorkelson, a travel writer currently living in Des Moines, is no longer obsessed with the World's Largest Cheeto. She's merely fond of it. Her stories about destinations in the Midwest and worldwide have appeared in magazines and newspaper travel sections, including the *Minneapolis–St. Paul Star Tribune,* the *Chicago Tribune,* and *Midwest Living* magazine.

Other books in the Curiosities Series